A TRIP INTO THE
SUPERNATURAL

Books by

Roger J. Morneau

A Trip Into the Supernatural
Incredible Answers to Prayer
More Incredible Answers to Prayer
When You Need Incredible Answers to Prayer
Beware of Angels

Videos

Incredible Answers to Prayer
A Trip Into the Supernatural

To order,
call **1-800-765-6955.**

For information on other products from
Review and Herald Publishing,
visit us at www.rhpa.org

ROBER J. MORNEAU

A TRIP INTO THE SUPERNATURAL

REVIEW AND HERALD® PUBLISHING ASSOCIATION
Since 1861 | www.reviewandherald.com

Printed with permission by Review and Herald® Publishing Association

This book was
Edited by Gerald Wheeler
Cover Design by Derek Knecht/Review and Herald® Design Center

Printed in U. S. A.
14th Printing
Printed in 2014

Library of Congress Cataloging in Publication Data
Morneau, Roger J., 1925-1998
A trip into the supernatural.
1. Morneau, Roger J., 1925-1998
2. Converts, Seventh-day Adventist—Canada—Biography.
3. Satanism. I. Title.
BX6189.M67A37 1982 248.2'46'0924 [B] 82-13280

ISBN 978-0-8280-2799-1

DEDICATION

I dedicate this book to a young lady who more than three decades ago gave me her hand and heart in marriage and was willing to share her life with me even if it meant walking under the shadow of death.

TO MY PRECIOUS WIFE—HILDA

ACKNOWLEDGMENTS

I have pleasure in acknowledging my debt of gratitude to Mrs. June Strong, who, as a professional writer, lent guidance and direction to my pen, and without whose help I would not yet have written what I know and feel about the matter of spiritual warfare.

Also, a word of thanks to Pastor William R. Lawson, who convinced me before I ever wrote the first sentence that I should record my experience with the spirits for the benefit of others.

I am also grateful to Ellen and Maynard Cady, who helped many times when the manuscript was being written, bringing my mind out of reliving the past by driving us through the mountains of Pennsylvania for a day at their mountaintop cabin.

Most of the names in this book have been changed to protect the privacy of those involved in the events depicted.

CONTENTS

Chapter 1

In Trouble With the Spirits

As I started to pick up a book to read, the piece of paper with the message on it to phone Roland began to levitate around the room; then it slapped against my open book with such force that it knocked the volume out of my hands and almost fell off my lap. My first impulse was to tell the spirit a thing or two, but I had determinded that regardless of what took place, I would not get involved in verbal communication with it. Placing the piece of paper between pages of the book, I continued to read. A short while later a force pulled the book out of my hands and threw it against the wall on the opposite side of the room.

Not because of the spirit's action, but because of respect for my friend, I decided to phone him. There was a pay phone in the hallway, but in this case I would not use it, so I went to a restaurant down the street. As I sat in the phone booth, I glanced at my watch: 1:00 a.m. The phone rang twice.

"Hello! Morneau, is this you?"

"Yes, it is."

"Morneau, you daredevil—what am I saying? I didn't mean it that way. I meant to say that you're gambling with your life. Have you lost your mind?"

"You sound upset," I replied. "What's your problem?"

"My problem? I have no problem. You're the one in great trouble and you sound as if you haven't got a care in the world. Morneau, I've always admired your daring spirit, but now you've gone too far—way too far. You've turned against the spirits that have benefited you, and now they will destroy you. I'm surprised that you're still alive. Man, I'm concerned about you. Because I care for your well-being, I've been sitting by this phone all evening waiting for your call. Don't you have anything to say?"

"Of course I have something to say, but how can I when you haven't given me a chance to talk?"

Immediately he continued, "Morneau, you don't understand the extent of the trouble you're in. By Wednesday evening—according to the Satanist priest—you were in deep trouble with the spirits. But now it's too late, too late."

"Roland," I interrupted, "if you'll calm down it will be much easier for us to understand each other. Now, explain yourself about Wednesday evening."

After a few moments he regained his composure. "Last Wednesday when I entered our place of worship, I was whisked into the high priest's office. He asked whether I had seen you in the past week. His expression gave me to understand that something awful had happened. I asked whether you were dead—maybe you had an accident. He stated that you were in a situation more horrible than that. On Tuesday night, during the sacred hour of midnight, a spirit counselor appeared to him and told him that you were studying the Bible with Sabbathkeepers—the very people the master hates most on the face of the earth. The priest asked me to try to get hold of you and make you realize the danger you're in, but I couldn't reach you."

"Everything is under control," I told him. "I'm in no great danger."

"That's what you think." His voice rose in pitch again. "At 6:30 this evening the high priest called to inform me that according to the spirits you have been in church today with those Sabbath people, and that has infuriated the master. What do you have to say about that?"

"Yes, I have been studying the Bible, and have gone to a Sabbath-observing church. But I couldn't care less about the way the fallen cherub feels about me. If you would like to know more about my activities during the past week, why don't you come over to see me in the morning?"

On my return home I prayed, then went to bed. Twenty minutes later the lights came on. I turned them off. Almost instantly they flashed back on. Then I decided to sleep with them on. A couple of minutes later almost everything started moving out of its place. A picture on a wall floated across the room and hung on the opposite wall, and a table lamp hung in midair without any visible support. As I observed the spirits' activities I realized that my prayers had placed them under some kind of restraint. They could not converse with me, as I believed they would have liked to do. Immediately I commanded them to leave by order of Christ Jesus. The lamp and pictures fell to the floor. Picking up the lamp, I straightened the damaged shade, but left the broken glass from the pictures, to be swept up in the morning. I thanked Jesus for His loving care over me, then returned to bed.

The thought that powerful demon spirits had left at His name filled me with a great sense of satisfaction. That encounter also served to strengthen my conviction that everything was—as I had told my friend—truly under control.

It must have been about an hour later when the spirits returned. Once more I compelled them, using Jesus' name, to leave my place. Without hesitation they departed, and I tried to get some sleep.

To my amazement, about 4:00 a.m. the irritating phenomena began again. Sitting in bed, I tried to figure out why the Lord had allowed them to come back. I concluded that perhaps I should hear for myself how demons felt about my acceptance of Jesus as my

Lord and Saviour.*

"So, you want to talk to me. OK, speak up."

"Why do you refuse to talk to us?" a spirit asked in a voice that drifted about the room.

"I have found a better Master."

"Why have you given us up when we have great wealth prepared for you?"

"You have deceived me for so many years that I have no use for you."

"We have treated you right since you affiliated with those who know the real source of wealth and power," he said in a voice that seemed to command respect and authority.

I perceived that I was conversing with a chief counselor. The very air in the place seemed charged with energy, and his presence was imposing. Realizing that I was no match for his power, I prayed silently, "Lord Jesus, please help me!" Then a passage of Scripture came to my mind—one that Pastor Taylor had brought to my attention that same day. "He came unto his own, and his own received him not. But as many as received him, to them gave he power to become the sons of God, even to them that believe on his name" (John 1:11, 12). Immediately I felt that God would carry me through that encounter victoriously. A great calm came over me. Later I realized my great danger in attempting to speak to spirits.

As our conversation continued I detected that the spirit seemed to be facing some kind of crisis. In fact I sensed waves of despair engulfing him as he became aware that he was wasting his efforts in trying to regain my allegiance.

"Listen to me carefully," the spirit said. "I am telling you the truth. The master has great wealth prepared for you if only you give up associating with the people he hates, and stop observing that Seventh-day Sabbath he despises."

"Spirit, I believe you're telling the truth, but I don't want your wealth. It's not enough. I have had a better offer for my allegiance—all the gold I want, plus unlimited life to enjoy it with. I have decided to turn my life over to Christ Jesus."

*Later I realized my great danger in attempting to speak to spirits.

"Stop mentioning that name," the spirit exploded. "I need to talk to you, but don't mention that name. I am a chief counselor. My spirit associates and I have worked to prepare the way so that the master could shower you with wealth. We have brought George the fame and honor he now enjoys. And we arranged for the two of you to meet so that you could understand what wonderful plans we have for your life. I plead with you—don't pass it up."

"Spirit," I said, "ten days ago I would have fallen for your line, but not today. Now I am what you could call an educated former demon worshiper. Jesus is now my Master, and with His help I will be a commandment keeper, joining those Sabbath observers you hate. As for you and your spirit friends, in reality you're a bunch of cheats. You offer me gold if I will forfeit eternal life. Forget it. I can wait for the coming of the Lord. Then I will possess all the gold I need in the earth made new."

For about two minutes, only my alarm clock ticking away broke the silence. Apparently the spirit counselor had met the unexpected. And as a losing general on a battlefield, he needed a little time to work out a new strategy.

"Very well," he said at last. "You are refusing wealth and fame from the master, so poverty shall be the lot of your life. That is, if you manage to stay alive any length of time. You will from this day on walk under the shadow of death."

Then followed a laugh such as I had never heard in my life. It conveyed an intense pleasure in cruelty. Immediately I thought that it must have been the type that Nero laughed as the lions pounced on Christian victims in the Roman arena. A shiver went up my spine, and I probably would have been terrified except for the assurance of God's protection.

"Spirit," I said, "I want you to know that I have placed myself in the care of the Christ of Calvary and that I am prepared to walk under the shadow of death as long as He goes with me. Now I command you in His name to depart from me and come no more."

A door leading to a back balcony opened as the spirit left, and slammed against the wall of the room with such force that the door handle almost went through the plaster.

Chapter 2

My Childhood Days

I was born the fifth child in a family of eight on April 18, 1925, in St. Jacques, New Brunswick, a small village near the border of the province of Quebec, in eastern Canada. My parents were devout French Catholics. On my father's side of the family, two of his sisters were nuns, and his younger brother a priest who later became a monseigneur of the Roman Catholic Church.

Even now I can't help admiring how my parents diligently followed the teachings and requirements of their church. As far back as I can remember, our home had daily family prayer. The evening prayer period I remember best. The Rosary was the main part of the service, but we also repeated the Litany of the Saints. It consisted in calling out the names of about 100 or more saints and asking them to pray for us. As children our knees became sore from kneeling so long a time. But we were encouraged to offer the suffering to God, that in turn He could use it to relieve some poor soul for a short while from the torment of the flames of purgatory.

Our family practiced many types of bodily humiliations in order to gain favor before God. Every Friday we abstained from meat. On the first Friday of every month if a person went to confession and received Communion, he was assured of indulgences that amounted to 5,000 days less in purgatory for a particular soul. In those days it meant taking no food or water from the evening before until after one had received Communion the following morning. (The church has since changed this rule.)

It was customary at certain times of the year for the members of our family to hold an all-night vigil. Each of us took turns kneeling for one hour before a statue and saying the Rosary or other prayers. The Lenten period, preceding Easter was also a time of great self-mortification. My parents were God-loving people, and all activities of their lives revolved around Him. To please God was their main objective.

When I was 3 years old, I became extremely sick and the doctors gave up on my getting well. In fact, my father made arrangements for my funeral. Then my mother promised God that if I became well again, she would do everything in her power to see that when I grew up I would be a priest, living to glorify His name and bring others to serve Him. According to her, an immediate improvement took place, and my recovery was rapid and complete.

The time came for me to prepare for my first Communion. The more I memorized of the catechism, however—the teachings and commandments of the church—the more difficult I found it to harmonize its teachings with what I knew of the gospel of Christ.

The priest read a chapter from either one of the four Gospels or one of the Epistles before his sermon on Sunday, and I always enjoyed it tremendously. Once when I was about 7 years old we were returning home from church one beautiful winter day. The sun shone brightly, and about 20 horse-drawn sleighs were following one another. The sound of all those bells on the sleighs didn't allow much conversation. Everyone rode along in silence. Then I broke it by asking my mother why Jesus was so kind to people when He walked on earth, and became so mean after He went to heaven?

"What makes you ask that?" she said.

"Why would a good God burn people in purgatory for hundreds of years over little offenses?" I inquired. "He certainly does not practice what He taught. You and Dad practice what you teach us—why doesn't He? You teach us to forgive one another's offenses. Shouldn't God also forgive completely?"

As I looked into her face, I could see that such reasoning puzzled her. My father tried to help her by appealing to higher authorities. "You see, son, it's like your uncle Felix the priest once said: God hates sin so much that to help people turn away from it He had to attach a great penalty to it. And besides, our Holy Father the pope knows of other good reasons why God uses purgatory, and we must not question the pope's authority."

Taught the transubstantiation doctrine, I accepted it as any other child of my age did, believing that in the Eucharist the priest changed the bread and the wine into the body and blood of Christ. But on Easter Sunday, 1937, the year my mother died, I heard something that led me to think differently.

The priest read from one of the Gospels about the resurrection of Christ. What fascinated me was the fact that Jesus had a hard time convincing His disciples that He was, in reality, resurrected—that He was a being with real flesh and bones, and not a spirit. A couple of interesting questions popped into my mind. Could it be that heaven is a real place, like on earth, where people with flesh and bones can live real lives, and not be spirits floating on clouds? But if Jesus is not a spirit, how can He be in the host?

It is probably difficult for some people to understand how

a small child could lose faith in God and turn against religion in the way I did. Perhaps I can explain what happened by recounting several incidents.

As a youngster what I heard and saw in the lives of adults impressed me deeply. Our home was a place where peace and joy abode. My parents gave us a good example of how people should get along together. They practiced kindness and consideration for others, and in turn expected us to forgive one another's shortcomings and be kind. Our parents were forever helping the poor and needy. In my estimation, I felt that God should at least be as kind and compassionate toward humans as He expected them to be toward each other.

One particular experience greatly perplexed my mind. In those days people did not use their cars during the winter months, and it sometimes took quite an amount of work to put a car back into running order for use during warmer weather.

My dad decided to have a mechanic who lived in Edmundston spend a couple of days getting his Model A Ford in condition. Before my father went to see the man he said, "The man is Protestant, but a very fine person and an excellent mechanic. Now, children, listen to me. It may well be that as we recite the Angelus at noon, before having our meal, that he will not participate in our devotions. Please, do not stare at him, and above all, don't ask embarrassing questions pertaining to his religion. You understand?" And as he spoke, he looked directly at me.

In unison we all replied, "Yes, Dad."

For three days the man worked on the car, and I enjoyed watching him. He was all that dad had told us, and more. A kind man, he seemed to enjoy talking to me. Nor did he use profanity.

My father owned and operated three farms, and, of course, employed quite a few men. Many times I heard him say, when he had decided to hire a new man, "Friend, I know that you and I will get along well together. I'm not hard to please. But one thing I want you never to forget. My wife and I don't allow people who work for us to blaspheme God or the saints. We have children whom we are trying to bring up to reverence God. So watch your words." Despite his request, they forgot themselves while working and called down all the saints from heaven with profanities.

But if the Protestant mechanic happened to skin his knuckles, or pinch his finger, all he said was "Ouch! That hurts!"

As for the Angelus, I found the mechanic to be more reverent than we were. When dad said, "Let us pray," he bowed his head, closed his eyes, and folded his hands. We never closed our eyes, and rushed through the Angelus as fast as possible.

After the man left, something troubled me greatly, and I could not put it out of my mind. It was a phrase I had memorized from the catechism: *"Hors de L'eglise Catholique Apostolique et Romaine il n'y a point de Salut."* Translated, it stated, "Outside of the Roman Catholic Church, there is no salvation."

My mother sensed that something was bothering me and asked about it. "Mother, where do the good Protestants go when they die ?"

"That is a good question, son. Why do you ask?" I quoted her what I had memorized from the catechism. She admitted she did not know, and suggested that we should ask my uncle when he came to visit us. My question must have also troubled her, for at the evening meal that day she told my father what we had talked about and asked his opinion on the subject.

He did not have much of an answer, but commented that he felt that God wouldn't leave a good person out of heaven, regardless of whether he was a Catholic or a Protestant. Probably, he suggested, when a good Protestant dies, the angels lead him through the back door. "Protestants do not have the glory of being welcomed by Saint Peter personally, but they shouldn't care as long as they get in. They shouldn't expect to be treated as celebrities. After all, their forefathers made a bad mistake when they left the Catholic Church, and all their descendants can expect to suffer on account of it."

While I concluded his reasoning was most likely correct, those solemn words kept running through my mind: "Outside of the Roman Catholic Church there is no salvation."

A few months went by and finally we heard that my uncle the priest would be visiting all the relatives. I asked my father if he could, when the opportunity presented itself, ask Uncle Felix about the good Protestants.

After we had visited for quite a while, dad turned to my uncle, and said, "Felix, tell me, where do the good Protestants go when they die?"

"Why do you ask?"

Dad explained my question in light of what the catechism said.

"What Roger has quoted to you from the catechism is correct," Uncle Felix replied. "There is no salvation outside of the Catholic Church regardless of whom the person may be."

His statement opened up quite a debate on the matter. My father claimed that it wouldn't be fair of God not to let a good Protestant into heaven, while my uncle took the heat out of the conversation by suggesting that the soul of a good Protestant probably went to Limbo at death. It is supposed to be the place where the souls of unbaptized infants go when they die. "One thing I do know," Uncle Felix concluded, "according to the church, no Protestant, good or bad, will go to heaven or will ever see God. And remember, I didn't make the rules; I only teach them. If there was any possible way for a Protestant to get to heaven, our Holy Father the pope surely would have told us."

The experience placed a big question mark in my mind about God's justice.

Time went by, and a couple of years later the matter of God's justice came up again.

One beautiful July evening someone passing by stopped to tell my parents that a neighbor had died suddenly while working about five miles from home. One statement disturbed everyone present: "He died without having a priest to give him the last sacrament of the church." After mentioning that the dead man's brother was bringing the body home, the man left, shaking his head from side to side while saying, "It's sad, sad, sad."

I can remember that incident as if it were yesterday. Before too long we saw a dilapidated horse-drawn wagon moving slowly down the road. A blanket covered the body, and the driver sat on the front of the wagon, legs dangling down, his face reflecting his despair.

A couple of neighbors who had come to use our phone (our family had one of the only two telephones for miles around) were sitting on the front porch with us. After the body had passed our house, my mother commented on how sad it was. "If only he could have had a priest to forgive his mortal sins so that he would not find himself going into hell fire. Let's hope he had only venial sins on his soul. That alone represents years of burning in the flames of purgatory."

"We'll have to get a few dollars together and have masses celebrated for the peace of his soul," my father said, "for I can't see how his widow and the kids will be able to do so."

One of the neighbors spoke up. "I feel like telling you to save your money. I am inclined to think that his soul is now in hell fire. You see, Mr. and Mrs. Morneau, this man was known to have had sticky fingers. What I mean to say is that he had at times taken things that were not his."

"That's a rather strong accusation," my father replied, "and unless you're able to prove it, I would appreciate your not saying anything at all."

"I hate to say this, but do you remember that last year about this time you were unable to locate a log-dragging chain you had bought only a short while before. If you were to go into his barn and look in one particular place, you would see your chain. I saw it there only a few days ago. As a matter of fact, I commented to the man about it; and he said that he had borrowed it from you, but that you did not know about it."

My father appeared shocked for a moment or two. But after regaining his composure he said, "This is quite a revelation to me. Listen everyone, I want you all to know that in the sight of God I am giving to the dead man the chain he had borrowed from me, even if he never had any intention of returning it. As a matter of fact, if he took anything else from me that I'm not aware of, I give it to him, also. In this way his soul is freed from any condemnation he may have brought upon himself in the sight of God."

"I don't mean to be irreverent toward God," the neighbor responded, "but right now I feel that you are kinder than He is. I must admit that this is the nicest gesture toward anyone I have ever seen or heard of. In fact, you may be the first human being ever to force God to take a soul out of hell fire and place him in purgatory till he is purified enough to enter heaven."

That experience made quite an impact upon me. For many days that incident kept passing through my mind. As I meditated upon it I agreed with the neighbor that my dad had a more noble character than the God he served. I concluded that God was most unkind in forcing souls to suffer in purgatory because the relatives had no money to have masses celebrated.

One experience that served to turn me completely against God was that of the passing away of my own mother. During the spring of 1937 my mother went to the hospital for an operation. After a couple of weeks they sent her home to live out her last days. Only 12 years old, I was at an impressionable age.

Arriving home from school one day, I went into her bedroom to kiss her on the forehead, which I did daily. "Please sit down," she said. "I would like to say something that I feel is important to both of us. As you know I have but a short while to be with you and I want you to remember this bit of advice. As you make your way through life, show appreciation to people for their kindness toward you. Give thanks to them even if it is only for a glass of water. People who express appreciation for small favors receive benefits in greater ways."

In those days it was customary to view the dead in their home instead of at a funeral parlor. For three days friends, relatives, and neighbors came to pay their respects and pray for my mother's soul. On the day of the funeral many felt that our mother was in heaven next to God because she had had so many Roseries recited for her. But that which made us feel best was the fact that my father had scheduled Gregorian masses for the peace of her soul.

As our uncle Felix explained to us, Gregorian masses have to be the most wonderful thing that can happen to someone's departed soul. He explained how Pope Gregory, who had a special concern for souls in purgatory, had devised them. The family arranges to have 300 masses celebrated at the same time in various parishes, convents, monasteries, etcetera on a particular day. According to him they have a redeeming power sufficient to take a soul directly to heaven, so that it would not even see the flames of purgatory.

That same day I heard a relative state that Gregorian masses cost one dollar each, or in other words, $300 for the entire arrangement. The thought entered my mind that we were most fortunate that our father could afford to help our mother get to heaven so nicely. Then I remembered a woman who had died six months earlier in our parish. Because the family was too poor to have any masses celebrated she would have to suffer in purgatory. Her funeral arrangements had upset my father greatly, since he was a member of the welfare committee of our parish.

Later in the day he sat down for his evening meal, then decided he would pass it up. My mother, sensing his mood, asked whether something was wrong. "Yes, I might as well tell you," he said. "I have spent the better part of the afternoon at the church presbytery with other members of the Welfare Committee discussing the problems of the poor in our parish. The main item of concern was the purchasing of a coffin for old Annie. I wasn't against trying to save a little money, but when Father Paquin asked the funeral director how much we would save if we had the crucifix and handles of the coffin removed before burial, I became upset and felt like giving the good father a piece of my mind. But I held back because of respect for his office. To put an end to the discussion, I said I would pay the difference in the cost. Things of this kind somehow get to me. It's a sad, sad thing to be poor in this day and age, especially when it comes to dying."

As I thought upon both incidents, I couldn't help feeling that God was most unjust by allowing the misery going on in our world to continue. As time went on, I lost confidence in God and the church and determined to have nothing to do with either as soon as I would be old enough to be on my own. In the fall of 1937 my father sent my brother Edgar and me to a boarding academy operated by the nuns of L'Hotel Dieu de St. Basil. I received a great deal more religious instruction that served only to further harden my heart. From outward appearances no one would have dreamed of the conflict going on in my soul. Step by step I turned away from God in disgust and hate. A few years went by, then World War II came along, and with it a call to serve my country.

Chapter 3

A Trip Into the Supernatural

The Canadian Merchant Navy attracted me because someone whom I knew had joined and told me how much he enjoyed it. Having the Royal Navy and Air Force watching over you (merchant shipping was the lifeline of the armed forces) gave you a secure feeling.

For two and one-half years I worked in the engine rooms of the various ships I was assigned to, most of the time as a fireman. I can remember coming on watch and saying to myself, "I hope no torpedo slams into these boilers while I stand here." A number of men whom I knew perished at sea. That merchant navy experience served to harden me more against God and man.

Good jobs were hard to find in Montreal after the war because thousands of discharged servicemen swarmed the city, looking for employment. I decided to learn a trade, something I could enjoy doing that would have some creativity to it. I didn't want a job just for the sake of earning a living. So I decided to take my time and make sure that when I decided on a particular choice I would really enjoy it.

Meanwhile, to occupy time I accepted a job at the Windsor Bowling Alleys located on Ste. Catherine Street West. At the time it was one of the nicest places in Montreal for that type of amusement. I was assistant to the manager of the billiard room. The work wasn't hard, I met a lot of people, and it was a good pastime.

I had not been employed there long when an old buddy I had sailed with at the beginning of my merchant navy experience came walking in. Delighted to find that both of us were still alive, we had dinner together that evening and talked about many things.

One topic that my friend Roland spoke about with great enthusiasm was his new interest in the supernatural. He told me how fortunate he was in having become acquainted with a group of people who were members of a society that communicated with the dead. The spiritualist medium had Roland talk with his father, who had died when he was only 10 years old. His father's spirit had given him much advice about the future.

While it was interesting to hear Roland's experiences with the supernatural, they gave me a weird feeling. Then he asked me whether I would be interested in attending one of their séances. "Maybe the medium could have you talk to the spirit of your dead mother. You would like that, wouldn't you?"

His enthusiasm abated some when he realized that I was so shocked that I could not answer. After a few seconds of silence he continued, "You wouldn't be afraid of talking to the departed soul of your dead mother, would you?"

Somehow I managed to say that I wouldn't, but I would like a little time to consider it, having never thought about such a thing before.

He looked me straight in the eyes and said, "Morneau, you're afraid. I can tell by the way you look at me—it's written all over your face. Man, you have changed a lot since I saw you last. The Roger Morneau I knew was afraid of nothing. I recall the time when you and I were deckhands along with six other neophytes, and the first mate came to us and said he needed a volunteer to go up and paint the upper portion of the mainmast the next day. 'Which one of you is willing to go up there?' he said. 'The height is not great—it's only 70 feet. But one has to have a lot of nerve once he has reached the top. He has to get off the board he sat on while being pulled up with a rope, and lie on his stomach across the top of the mast [it was two feet in diameter] in order to paint on the opposite side.' All of us were scared to death to go up there, and we were delighted to hear you tell the first mate that you would. Talk about courage, fellow, you had it. Now, tell me, you're not going to chicken out on coming with me to our next séance, are you?"

After that little speech I couldn't refuse. Suddenly I had to live up to the image of Roger Morneau being afraid of nothing. I was hooked.

Thus one Saturday evening my friend and I found ourselves in a home where a visiting medium was to be an honored guest, and we were introduced to some of the others present. One couple in particular we felt honored to meet. The man was a professional entertainer, a jazz band leader currently in great demand. His band played in the most elegant night spots.

Late that evening after the séance concluded and some of the guests prepared to leave, the band leader turned to his wife and said, "Honey, what do you say that we depart, as it's getting late?"

At the moment she was conversing with the medium, whom she found most interesting. "George, why don't you go home and get your rest," she replied, "and I'll stay a little while longer and have the Belangers drive me home?" He agreed with her suggestion and proceeded out of the house just as Roland and I left.

Once outside George turned to us and said, "You fellows driving?"

"No, we're going to take the streetcar about two blocks from here," I said.

"I'll be glad to drive you there. Jump in."

During the evening the subject had come up that both of us had been in the merchant navy during the war. The spirit medium had conjured the (supposed) spirit of one of Roland's coworkers who had perished when the ship they were on sank.

As we entered George's automobile, he began to ask about the dangers of our work during the war. But in no time at all we had reached our destination. He then made a suggestion.

"What do you say that we go to a restaurant and have a bite to eat, and at the same time you could tell me about your adventures during the war? They fascinate me. It will be my treat. Then I'll drive you home."

George drove to Ste. Catherine Street West, an area known by the natives as the gourmet restaurant section of Montreal. Suddenly he steered his deluxe Lincoln into a narrow drive leading to the rear of one of his favorite eating spots, then left the car parked behind a black Cadillac, saying, "Joe is here. He's the owner of the place, a fine fellow."

When we entered the place, a hostess informed us that we would have to wait in the lounge until a table became available. As we headed there Joe spotted George from quite a distance away and came over to greet him.

Informed that we were waiting for a table, Joe stated that we wouldn't have to. A telephone call a couple of minutes earlier had just cancelled a reserved table. It was ours for the taking. We followed the owner, who removed the reserved sign from the table and sat us down.

The cocktail waitress came over and took our order for drinks. She said that we might have to wait a little longer than usual for our food to reach us because the place was filled to overcapacity. George asked for a double in his favorite alcoholic beverage in order to occupy time. Then we answered his questions about the merchant navy and talked of our interest and activities with the supernatural.

A fair amount of time elapsed until our food came, and we consumed a second order of drinks. It put George in a talkative mood, which in turn made him willing to tell us many things that I doubt he would have mentioned under normal circumstances. For instance, I asked whether he would tell us a little about how he became so famous in his profession.

"I don't mind at all," he said. "As a matter of fact, I'll tell you the real and true reason of my success, something my wife doesn't even know about. But you must promise to keep it in strict confidence."

We assured him that whatever he mentioned would remain a secret.

"You fellows know anything about demon worship?"

"I don't," I answered. "Why do you ask?"

Without answering my question, he inquired, "How long have you fellows been involved with sorcery?"

"George, I don't understand what you're getting at. What do you mean?"

"What I mean to say is, How long have you been pretending to hold communication with the dead?"

"Not very long for me," I replied.

"I see where you guys have a lot to learn when it comes to the supernatural. You're both wasting your time by going to those spiritualistic séances. Don't get me wrong, they have their place. They're a good pastime for women in that they receive some comfort from thinking that they're getting guidance in their lives through some departed loved one. You see, the reason I attended the séance this evening was just to make my wife happy. I go with her a couple of times a year to make her feel that I'm concerned with her interests—that's the only reason. What she doesn't know is that I have learned to go to the very source of that power, where a person can get real action—demon worship, that is."

Of all that he had said to us, one sentence stood out in my mind. "George, would you clarify the question you asked us a little while ago: 'How long have you been pretending to hold communication with the dead?' What do you mean by the word *pretending?*"

He smiled, glanced at his watch, and said, "It's too late to explain that one tonight, but let me tell you this—you have not been talking with the dead." Then he went back to discussing his personal success.

"You see, for years it seemed I was a failure in organizing and maintaining my own jazz band. Then I was fortunate enough to be introduced to demon worship. And by that great power I have obtained everything I had always wanted. Of course, I had to become acquainted with certain rituals that I needed to perform before the spirits began to work things out in my behalf."

His face lit up with a big smile. "From that day on, it was instant success for me and my band. Recognition came to us overnight. Without any effort on our part we were discovered (though we had been there all the time) and heralded as one of the great bands in our field. Somehow the news media got all excited about us. We became the talk of the town. The leading people of the radio world discussed us, and in no time we reached the top."

George took another sip from his glass, a puff from his cigarette, and continued. "We have been in constant demand ever since. Money flows in. Our fees are the highest in the industry. People like to dance to our music. In reality, the spirits take control of us—or in other words, possess us, energize us—and in turn we pass the influence on to the people. They like what they get and keep returning for more of the same."

Leaning back and lighting another cigarette, he chuckled a little and said, "You guys have got to hear this. I had an interview on radio about a month ago and I really enjoyed myself. There were six of the top people of the radio world from Montreal and Toronto conversing with me. Everything I said seemed to fascinate them. In fact, I was amazed over my instant responses. Never had I been so witty in my life. And I enjoyed the attention they gave me. It almost reached a state of worship. In addition, they were trying to figure me out. And when we parted, they still hadn't succeeded."

Looking at his watch once more, he said, "Fellows, it's getting very late. What do you say that we get rolling for home?"

Waiting to get his check, George commented, "That success of mine is easy to figure out once a person understands the mighty power of the spirits and the process involved in getting that power to working for you."

Amazed at what he had told us, Roland and I asked him to tell us more about it as we drove home.

"I feel impressed to tell you of my experience because I believe you're looking for something powerful to benefit your lives. And I know that you will not find it by attending séances such as the one you were at this evening. Let me put it to you this way: Why do you want to play in the little leagues when you can be in the majors?"

My friend then asked him to tell us how to get into the major leagues of the spirit world.

"You two are truly brave young men," George said, "and have done a lot for our country. Now I'm going to do something great for you. I will arrange to have you both attend our next spirit worship assembly."

Then George, glancing from side to side, an air of indecision about him, finally said, "There is one point I want to assure myself of. I presume you have no reverence for Christ in your life—am I right? The reason I ask is that we can't have anyone there who has any loyalty to the Christian God, as it could be disastrous."

We both assured him that we had blasphemed God, and gone past the point of no return.

"I became aware of that fact this evening," he continued, "in that the conjured spirits seemed to favor you two above all the people present there. I hope that my question did not offend you. I had to ask it just to make doubly sure that you guys are *OK.*"

Although I was somewhat reluctant to attend a gathering of demon worshipers, my friend Roland had no hesitation in doing so. He reasoned that, since we were going to hell anyway to burn throughout eternity, we might as well get acquainted with some of the folks before we arrived.

I assumed that George might never contact us again, since he had been drunk when he made the invitation and in the morning probably would not even remember half of what he had said the night before. But a few days later we both received a call to be ready at 8:00 the following evening, when he would pick us up.

That ne'er-to-be-forgotten evening began by George filling us in on many details of the secret society to which he belonged. He wasn't a fast driver and seemed reluctant to pass streetcars in motion. We must have made probably a hundred stops on our way to the meeting. So we had a lot of time to converse before we reached our destination.

George told us that we should not be surprised to meet some of the great and successful people of Montreal, and named at least a half dozen of the more notable ones. His statement surprised me in that I had already concluded that we would meet a group of tough-looking characters. But on the contrary, everyone was surprisingly well mannered, superbly dressed, and possessed a winning personality. They made us feel as if they had known us for a long time and we were part of the group.

The meeting convened about 15 minutes after our arrival. It was most informal. The people spent about two hours telling of the fantastic accomplishments they had attained through the workings of the spirits—mainly business transactions resulting in great profits to themselves as the result of their abilities to use clairvoyance and mental telepathy (by way of the spirits) to influence people in their decisions.

One man told of how, as an astrologer using divination, he became a counselor to certain wealthy persons in their investments, and was himself becoming rich. He explained how a demon spirit hovered at his side during each session to give him precise information—audible to him, but not the client—on how they should invest and when. "These rich folks have the means to invest," he said. "I have the know-how to make it pay off."

Highly impressed, my friend asked whether he ever worried about being cheated on his share of the returns?

"I counsel on a percentage of the returns on investments. As you are well aware, the astrology bit is only a come-on. I have no worry. My familiar spirit looks out for my well-being. Let me illustrate.

"One couple tried to deprive me of my fair share of one profitable industrial real estate transaction. They presented me with a check making up quite a bundle, and I felt satisfied, until my familiar spirit told me to ask them when they were going to give me the additional $1,700 that made up my correct share of the profits on that particular investment. The wife fainted, and the husband was terrified. He quickly explained that they had no intentions to cheat me and the money would be in my hands within 24 hours."

After each success story, the individual would always praise or give credit to a particular spirit by name, and many times referred to the spirit as lord of his life.

During the time I was involved with demon worshipers, I observed that in their testimonies of how the spirits had worked for them, they often referred to a demon as "lord god." For instance, one would say, "It was wonderful to see the lord god Beelzebub's power exhibited in my behalf on such and such a day." Or someone would ask, "Sam, how have you been since I saw you last?" The reply would be, "Real fine, thank you. The gods have really benefited my life in wonderful ways."

That evening one individual impressed me greatly. A medical doctor, he explained how the spirits had given him great hypnotic and healing powers, including the ability to take away pain and to stop bleeding in wounds and severe cuts.

After telling some fascinating accounts of his healing people, he announced he must go down to the worship room. "Will you, friends, please excuse me?" he said. "I need to go and perform acts of devotion so as to be regenerated by the lord god Nehushtan. I depend on his vivifying power to revive and heal my patients."

An hour after the meeting started, a latecomer appeared. A number of people greeted him, referring to him as Charmer. As we drove back home late that evening, I asked George, "What about that dignified looking gentleman who came in late? Some addressed him as Charmer. Does the name have any particular significance?"

"It does, but I can't say anything about him now. After you have attended a few of our meetings and you become part of the group, remind me to tell you about him. He's a fascinating individual. In fact, he is believed among us to have been the greatest charmer, or hypnotist, who has ever walked the sidewalks of Montreal.

"By the way, fellows, I was delighted to see how everyone this evening took to you guys. It made me feel good to see that. Understand this: We are a closely knit group. In fact, I had a hard time getting permission to bring you with me to this meeting. At first I was refused the privilege. Then through the working of a spirit counselor appearing to our leader on vacation in the U.S.A., I received a phone call giving me the OK, and the way opened for you to associate with us and eventually become members of our society. I'll tell you more about it sometime in the future."

I felt somewhat uncomfortable when I heard George assuming that I was going to become one of them. But the whole thing overjoyed Roland.

"After a few visits," George said, "I'll have you come downstairs to see our worship room. I think you will find it quite impressive. However, it will not be possible for you to visit the worship room of the gods until the Satanist priest is present, and only then after receiving the approval of the spirits."

The meeting had taken place in a private home, a luxurious Montreal residence. As we visited on the main floor, we could hear, faintly coming from the basement level, sounds that closely resembled the type of religious music and chanting used by the people of India. Every so often some of the people would go downstairs, returning about 30 minutes or so later. All that activity prompted George to lean toward me as we sat on a sofa, saying softly, "Our worship room is downstairs. I'll tell you about it after we leave this evening."

About six weeks after we had met the man called Charmer, I asked George one evening as we were returning home whether he felt like telling us about him.

"Oh, yes, you fellows should hear about that fascinating individual. But first I would like to remind you that we are, generally speaking, a law-abiding group of citizens. I don't know of any one of us who wouldn't give the shirt off his back to help someone. And we never really take advantage of people with the powers the spirits have passed on to us.

"But in the case of the Charmer—well, he's somewhat different from the rest of us. It appears that he has a weakness in his character and, because of it, employed his great hypnotic power, or gift, in a way that he should not have done. I should say that he lost his sense of direction for a short while.

"He is a sharp businessman—owns two nightclubs—and has been doing exceedingly well. And as I said before, he's a powerful hypnotist. He can place a person under his spell, or in a hypnotic trance, in less than ten seconds if he or she agrees to look him straight in the eyes.

"Having two nightclubs, he has a lot of contact with show business people. Most groups stay for an engagement about four to six weeks, then move on to another area. We became aware of the fact that some of the groups were breaking up or would lose one of their members after performing in one of his clubs. And the dropout was always female. About six months ago the Montreal vice squad raided a plush house of prostitution where all the girls consisted of former nightclub entertainers, and every one of them had worked for him.

"You see," George continued, "those girls would never have found themselves in the situation they were in if they had not agreed to let someone hypnotize them. Such a person can never from then on resist the hypnotist's power."

Chapter 4

Worship Room of the Gods

During Roland's and my third visit to a demon worshipers assembly George informed us that the Satanist priest would be present, having just returned from a trip to the States. He felt quite sure that the priest would look favorably upon us, and undoubtedly would have us visit the worship room of the gods.

When we came in, we were introduced to a couple of persons we had not met before, then began to chat with a few people who came to wish us a good evening. Shortly afterward the priest entered. Shaking people's hands and speaking a few words to them, he slowly moved in our direction. When he reached us George said, "Reverend, I would like you to meet a couple of fine gentlemen."

We conversed with him for a while, during which he surprised us both by some of the things he said. For instance, when George commented that we had been in the merchant navy, the priest mentioned the names of the ships we had been on, plus a couple of details known to no one else. I must admit that it made quite an impression on us. He then excused himself and, as he did, stated that he would appreciate having a short talk with us sometime during the evening.

Not only his words but his very presence reflected an air of mysterious secrecy. He had piercing eyes, a bald head, and a deep, low voice which he accompanied by an occasional chuckle as he talked. His physical size alone overwhelmed one. I would say that he was equal in size to the late general Charles de Gaulle.

After quite a lengthy testimonial session to the gods, the priest again joined us in friendly conversation. He informed us that the spirits had acquainted him with much concerning us and had manifested their desire to benefit our lives by bestowing great gifts upon us.

When most of the people had left he invited us to visit the worship room of the gods.

For you to understand better how startling and almost shocking the revelations were that I would soon receive, I must describe the mental image my Catholic upbringing had established in my mind about the devil and his fallen angels. Adults had taught me during my childhood that the devil and his angels are in hellfire in the middle of the earth, attending to the never-ending task of imposing various types of tortures upon the souls of those who died in a state of mortal sin. The adults represented demons to us children as being half human and half animal, having horns and hoofs and breathing out fire. As I entered my teens, I concluded that the whole idea was ridiculous, that it was most likely an invention of some overactive mind during centuries past who wanted to exploit the superstitious and uneducated. I eventually questioned the existence of such beings as the devil and his angels.

We proceeded downstairs with the priest, who seemed delighted to take us on a tour of their sanctuary. As we went along he kept telling us how a spirit had drawn the architectural designs for the place.

He pointed out the intricate works of great beauty along the grand staircase. Even today I still remember the carvings adorning its massive banister, the splendid wall decorations, and the huge chandelier over the first landing.

The spacious sanctuary struck me with awe. An air of mysterious secrecy filled the place, giving the impression that great intelligence had been at work to fascinate the human mind so it would respond in reverence and submission without asking questions.

The rooms were sumptuous and magnificent. Gold was everywhere. The lighting fixtures and many other objects were plated or trimmed in the metal. The priest said that some things were even of solid gold. Although the place was not brightly lit, it was done in a way that the golden objects seemed to glow with great splendor.

But I believe that the abundance of beautiful oil paintings arrested my attention most. About 75 paintings of about 48 by 30 inches hung on the walls.

The Satanist priest mentioned that if we had any questions he would be happy to answer them.

"Who are the noble-looking individuals portrayed in those paintings?" I asked.

"They are the gods you have heard folks talk about in the testimonial sessions. The chief counselors, they rule over legions of spirits. After they materialized to let us photograph them, we had paintings made of them. Because they deserve such great honors, we have placed right below each painting a small altar, making it possible for people in their devotions to burn candles and incense and to perform such rituals as the spirits request."

As we slowly moved along we came to an altar upon which rested a staff with a brass serpent coiled around it. The priest mentioned that the altar was dedicated to the god Nehushtan, whose power the physician we had heard on our first visit had put wonderfully to work. He commented about the great miracles performed by the god of brass for the children of Israel when they burned incense before the brazen serpent that Moses had made centuries earlier (see 2 Kings 18:4).

At the end of the room stood a large altar with a life-size painting of a majestic-looking individual above it. To my friend's inquiry, the priest replied, "It is dedicated to the master of us all."

"What do you call him?" I asked.

His face took on an expression of pride. "God with us."

Today, as I recall that painting, having many times admired it, I must say that the individual portrayed had features that reflected a superior intellect. He had a high forehead, piercing eyes, and a posture that gave one the impression of his being a person of action, possessing great dignity.

The priest's answer was not what I had expected, and it was not really clear. Surely he could not be referring to Christ Jesus. No, it could not be. But could it be . . . ?

"Do you mean to say that this painting is a true image of Satan?" I managed to say at last.

"Yes, it is, and you probably wonder where the hideous animal-like characteristics have gone." Chuckling, he added, "Pardon me for laughing a bit. Please believe me, I am not laughing at you gentlemen over your bewildered state of mind. In reality I am delighted and amused at the thought that the demon spirits have been so clever in concealing their true identity, that even in this age of scientific advancement and great learning, a vast majority of Christians still believe in the horn-and-hoof theory."

Then his facial expression changed to reflect an air of deep concern as he said, "It is most solemnly important today that the up-and-coming generation be lead to believe that the master and his spirit associates do not really exist. Only in this way will they be able to rule the inhabitants of this planet successfully for the decades just before us."

An expression of confidence crossed his face. "Nothing so

intrigues the spirits as to devise ways to make humans into members of Satan's coming kingdom."

While we were looking at the various altars and paintings, the high priest explained that demon spirits are in reality specialists in various fields of activity. Having a background of experience measured in millenniums, they are engaged in a fierce conflict for the control of men's minds, a conflict against the forces from above.

When Roland wondered why the spirits were spending so much effort to deceive humanity, the priest stated that everyone they could make to disqualify himself from being a member of Christ's kingdom automatically became a member of Satan's great kingdom that he would before long establish on earth. Those who went down into the grave under Satan's leading he would someday restore to life. Christ and His followers, he said, intended to end the intense struggle between the two great forces by raining fire from heaven up on Satan's followers, but it would not hurt them, because demon spirits could now control fire so it had no power to burn human beings. And he added that if I doubted what he was saying, I could go to India or other areas of the world that had perfected black magic to a science and I would behold fire walkers stepping across a bed of coals without so much as singeing a hair of their legs.

As we left the worship room I stated that I felt quite confused about Satan and his angels. My Catholic upbringing had taught me that Satan and his angels were in hellfire with the souls of people who had died in the state of mortal sin. What was the truth ?

The Satanist priest agreed to take time to give us what he called a true picture of things. "Gentlemen, I realize that your visit to our worship room has raised questions in your minds. First, let me tell you that we, the members of our secret society here in Montreal, are the elite of spirit worshipers. When the struggle between the forces from above and those of our great master comes to an end and he permanently establishes his kingdom on this planet, we will receive high positions of authority and honor. We will be richly rewarded for having sided with what now appears to be the underdog—if you get what I mean.

"Millenniums ago our great master had jurisdiction over countless numbers of beings in a vast universe. He became misunderstood and was forced to flee his domain along with the other spirits who sympathized with him.

"The inhabitants of this planet welcomed our master kindly. But as the result of his superior intellect, he became the rightful possessor of the planet by causing the original owners to forfeit their right to it by believing something that he said was in reality factual. Some people may call this deception, but he was merely following the law of self-survival, a natural instinct in all great leaders.

"When it became known that his rival—Christ—would come to earth after assuming the nature of man to attract humanity to Himself, our master and his chief counselors decided to follow a strategy similar to the one that originally had enabled them to acquire their new dominion.

"This planned course of action would require all demon spirits to carefully counsel humans to live in a way that would disqualify themselves from becoming members of Christ's kingdom. The spirits would encourage people to listen to their feelings instead of the word of Christ and His prophets. In no surer way could the spirits obtain control of people's lives without the individuals realizing what was happening. The spirits would suggest all kinds of erroneous doctrines and ideas, and humanity would readily accept them because they felt strongly about them."

The high priest, his face radiating his fascination with what he had just told us, asked for permission to take a few additional minutes of our time to illustrate what he had talked about. When we assured him of our deep interest, of our desire to know more about the activities of the spirits, he continued.

"If you recall, gentlemen, Solomon, the king of Israel, had been gifted with great wisdom and had attracted the attention of a number of powerful rulers. At the same time, our great master became concerned over Solomon's getting all that attention and decided that he should make a supreme effort to control the entire world. Up to then he had succeeded in establishing idolatry in every part of the world, except in the nation of Israel. So it was decided that certain spirit counselors should first cause Solomon to think highly of himself. Second, they should lead him to feel strongly that it would be in the best interest of his nation to form alliances with the surrounding nations, even though many of his advisors would urge him not to do so.

"Our master's plan was a huge success. When the day came that by Solomon's example Israel worshiped Ashtoreth, the goddess of the Zidonians; Chemosh, the god of the Moabites; and Milcom, the god of the children of Ammon [1 Kings 11:33]—when the people prostrated themselves before idols representing demon spirits—our master felt that his triumph was complete. He had reached his great objective. The whole world was in reality at his command.

"Gentlemen, I believe that by now you realize the master's great wisdom and cleverness in concealing his true identity. It assures his dedicated agents that their diligence will be rewarded some day when they see the generations of earth standing before them in humble obedience, acknowledging that their master is in reality a great god."

"The great master," he continued, "leaves nothing to chance. With well-matured plans and great care he lays his snares to captivate the minds of millions of the wisest mortals and thus secure their allegiance both in this present life and for eternity."

Vibrant with enthusiasm for Satan's cause, the man proceeded to tell us about what he called "the most awesome assembly of spirit beings ever to converge in one place on the face of this planet."

"At the beginning of the eighteenth century," he said, "Satan and his spirit counselors held a great general council to prepare for the industrial age that would soon break upon the world. Satan foresaw that an age of scientific discovery and intellectual enlightenment would immediately follow upon its heels. It would usher in the end-times, the close of the struggle between the forces of good and evil.

"Since Satan had been studying the prophecies of the Bible, he understood the meaning of Daniel 12:4 that described the time of the end, how many shall run to and fro, and how knowledge would be increased. He recognized it as an ideal time to separate humans from their Creator, thus leading earth's multitudes to perdition. It offered a sure way to build up his coming kingdom to such an extent that few people will be left to leave this planet when Christ comes for them in a secret rapture at the close of the Christian Era."

In an aside the priest boasted that Christ would not really return to Earth in power and glory, but would abdicate all claims to the planet, knowing that it was legally and rightfully Satan's. "Then the great master will resurrect our people from their graves, and establish his own unending kingdom here.

"After lengthy deliberations," he said, returning to the subject of Satan's general council, "it closed after having produced plans for deceptions that would disqualify vast numbers of people from Christ's kingdom. They would then automatically become part of Satan's kingdom. The executive committee had adopted a three-part plan.

"The first part would be to convince human beings that Satan and his angels did not really exist.

"The second part sought to obtain total control over people by introducing hypnotism as a new and beneficial science. Men of great learning," the priest explained, "would, under the direction of friendly spirits, perpetuate the doctrine of the immortal soul by causing people under their hypnotic spell to supposedly regress in time to former lives. Such individuals would vividly describe historical events that they otherwise knew nothing about when not in a trance.

"And to add power to the deception," the spiritist priest continued, "at times the spirits would cause the hypnotized person to speak fluently a foreign language he or she had not previously known. This would help Satan de-Christianize the Western world through the avenue of mysticism.

"The third part of Satan's plan would destroy the Bible without actually doing away with it. Satan would drive the thought of God out of the minds of millions through the theory of evolution."

The priest claimed that Satan had selected individuals of great intellect to advance his plan. "He chose an Austrian physician named Franz Mesmer to transform hypnotism from a plaything of the occult into a new science. Mesmer originated a theory called animal magnetism. Spirits led him to believe that a mysterious fluid penetrates the human body and allows certain persons to have a powerful influence over others.

"By the time he died in 1815 hypnotism as an anesthetic had begun to acquire an aura of respectability among many European physicians. They discovered that their medical practice now seemed more effective than ever before."

Pausing, a big smile on his face, the priest added, "They had no idea that they were actually being energized by friendly spirits.

"Satan's plan to destroy the Bible without actually getting rid of it has to be the most clever thing I have ever heard of," he laughed. "Charles Darwin, born in 1809, and Thomas Henry Huxley, born in 1825, both came under the influence of spirits at an early age because medical doctors used hypnotism as a form of anesthetic.

"The spirits decided that when the two children became adults, they would be the instruments to advance the religion that we know as the theory of evolution. By tying it in with the scientific revolution breaking across the world most people would never even recognize that it was a religion—a religion that crossed all denominational boundaries and even caught up the nonreligious.

To my shock and amazement, the priest then claimed that "the spirits consider anyone who teaches the theory of evolution to be a minister of that great religious system, and the individual will receive a special unction from Satan himself. Satan gives him great power to induce spiritual blindness, to convince, and to convert. In fact, he holds such people in such high regard that he assigns a special retinue of angels to accompany him or her all his or her life. It is the greatest honor that Satan can bestow upon a person in the presence of the galaxy."

The priest explained that Satan and his counselors had concluded that they could use the theory of evolution to destroy the very foundation of the Bible. "They could turn it against the Creation week, the Fall, and the plan of redemption. The stakes were so high here that the spirits tell us that Satan himself tutored Charles Darwin in setting up the principles of his scientific concepts."

With obvious pride the priest next explained how spirits can take a person of seemingly no importance and elevate him or her to positions of honor and respect. This person's name can even become immortal. "A good example," he said, "is Thomas Henry Huxley, who, until the spirits intervened, was nothing more than a surgeon in the British navy. They enabled him to become famous as a zoologist, lecturer, and writer. He accomplished marvels in making Darwin's theory acceptable to the public even though he introduced the idea that man is a descendant of apes.

"Having once been a Catholic priest," our guide concluded, "I say that it is impossible for someone to believe in the biblical Creation week, the Fall, and the plan of redemption, and at the same time hold to evolution. Such a hodgepodge of ideas has to be the greatest form of blasphemy known to the Creator."

(By the way, I should mention that this society of spiritists never referred to God as such, but always to the Creator. They spoke only of Satan and his angels as gods.)

By now something puzzled me. "How in the world can anyone consider evolution as a religious doctrine?" I asked. "Everybody knows it's just a theory, something assumed because it seems the best way of explaining how life apparently originated on earth."

The man's eyes gleamed with additional excitement as he replied, "A religious doctrine is anything that brings a person closer to his god. It may be a concept, an activity, or even something that may appear totally unrelated to religion. But if it serves to promote the ideals of Satan, the great god of this world, it is indeed a religious doctrine in the fullest sense of the word. In fact, I got this definition directly from a spirit counselor."

After I accepted Jesus as my Saviour, I began studying the Bible to see how a belief in evolution might disqualify a person from God's kingdom. I began to understand why as I considered Jesus' words about blasphemy against the Holy Spirit (see Matt. 12:31, 32).

You see, when someone declares that he or she can no longer believe in God's creation, that we cannot take the concept of the Fall of the human race seriously, and that human beings are little more than highly evolved animals, then that individual is in a very real sense accusing the Holy Spirit of being a lying spirit. Since the Bible was written under the direct inspiration of the Holy Spirit, he or she is charging that the Spirit is untrustworthy.

After we conversed a short while longer with the spiritist leader, he asked, "Do you have any more questions that you would like answered?"

While we had been looking at the paintings, I had observed that Satan's altar seemed to be solid marble, approximately nine feet in length, 36 inches in height, and about 30 inches wide. "The master's altar appears to be one solid block," I observed. "How did you get so heavy an object down there?"

The priest smiled. "You are very observant, Mr. Morneau. Or could it be that the master has impressed that observation on your mind so he can reveal to you his great power? By the way, young men, one of the spirit counselors has told me that the master has a very special purpose for the lives of both of you. So let me tell you of the spirits' power. But first, do you mind if I light a cigar?"

We were at the time sitting on the sofas by a picture window that gave us a beautiful view of the city bathed in a sea of light. I got the impression that the priest greatly enjoyed telling us about the main interest of his life—the activities of the demon spirits. And we had the time to listen.

"The master's altar was brought to its present location in the same manner and by the same power that Druid priests employed to erect the Stonehenge structures—spirit power, or in other words, the process of levitation. The spirits have revealed to me the great accomplishments of Druid priests among the ancient Celts in France, England, and Ireland more than 28 centuries ago. I was shown that at the hours of noon and midnight, during the full moon, the Druids levitated blocks of gray sandstone, weighing as much as 28 tons, into precise position to erect their places of worship."

He then took a couple of puffs on his Churchill cigar, sat back, and continued. "Aware of their accomplishments, I felt that the same privilege was mine to exercise and enjoy. Therefore I notified my people of my intentions to give the master a token of our affections in a beautiful altar. They felt that if I had the faith to believe that the spirits would set the altar in its designated place, they would take care of the cost and transportation to the rear entrance of our place of worship. Without hesitation I told them to place an order for an altar made of white Carrara marble. Nothing is too good for the master.

"I know by experience that the spirits' power has no limit

when it comes to working for those who believe the word of the master. And they greatly rewarded my faith when, during our midnight devotional service, the gods levitated that marble altar to its resent location.

"By the way, gentlemen, you have been greatly honored this evening, although you may not be aware of it. As we stood by the master's altar looking at that beautiful painting, which is in reality but a faint expression of his beauty and glory, the master appeared to me and stood by the far end of the altar for about three minutes, listening to us talk. That is why I suggested that we bow in the manner that we did. Your complying with my request brought, I could tell, great joy to the master's heart.

"It may interest you to know that we have not been aware of the master's presence in our midst for almost three months, as a result of the fact that the United Nations has been fashioning peace plans. That is requiring the master's undivided attention, a work that he dares not commit to anyone else.

"Peace on earth is not in the best interest of his kingdom, so he has the mammoth task of delegating to his legions of spirit agents what they must do to perplex and keep personal feelings running high among humanity's leaders. The problems the spirits raise will have these leaders always searching for solutions so they won't have time to get together."

Of all that I had heard, one point stood out above everything else: the statement that Satan's painting but faintly expresses his beauty and glory. I decided to bring the subject up again. Using the terminology that I thought correct at the time, I asked, "Reverend, would you clarify something you said? I'm sure I have not grasped fully what you meant." I then repeated it and waited for his reply.

"Yes, friends, the painting of the master but dimly reveals him. When a spirit materializes, it usually hides the beauty and glory that it possesses in its natural state of being. If a spirit would make itself visible to us right now without shielding us from its brightness, we could not look upon it without hurting our eyes.

"For instance, while on my recent vacation in the U.S.A. a chief counselor appeared in my hotel suite in Chicago. He had come with the urgent message that the person I had left in charge here was about to wreck all the work the spirits had done to bring you in touch with our society. But I'll tell you more about that in the near future. Anyway, his brightness was so dazzling that I could not gaze upon him. After giving me a few words of advice he left. But the shock of that light left me partially blinded for about 30 minutes. A few minutes later I tried to dial a call, but couldn't make out the numerals on the phone. I had to ask the operator for assistance."

We conversed a little longer with the priest, who filled us in on many points regarding demon worship. Then before we left that evening he swore us to secrecy concerning what we had seen and heard.

The high priest spoke an incantation, parts of which we repeated after him, and we sealed the pact by depositing a pinch of powdered incense slowly above the flame of a black candle, causing it to burn intensely and filling the room with a rich aroma.

After returning to my residence, I found myself unable to sleep all night, since I could not stop thinking about the worship room visit. The idea that Satan and his angels do indeed exist and are actually beautiful beings—not hideous creatures—I had a hard time adjusting to. My Catholic upbringing had warped my mind so badly from reality that I had great difficulty accepting it. It took about two months of supernatural manifestations before I accepted the fallen angels for what they are—beautiful, superintelligent beings.

Chapter 5

Spirits in Action

About two or three weeks after visiting the worship room I had another opportunity to discuss Satan and his angels with the high priest. When I mentioned to him that I had expected to meet a group of tough-looking characters he smiled and chuckled a little. "Spirit worshipers, like members of any society, vary greatly. Often they reflect the local culture. As you travel you will notice that among people with large illiteracy, superstition prevails. They will employ the most degrading forms of worship. The spirits in such cases delight in leading people that way because they know it hurts their great Rival, Christ. He claimed that He would draw all men to Himself. But the spirits have proven Him wrong, over the centuries, innumerable times. Millions upon millions have gone to the grave without so much as having ever heard of His name, much less believing in Him."

As the priest talked he rose from his desk chair and began pacing the floor. He folded his hands behind his back and kept staring at the floor, occasionally glancing up at me.

"As for us here in Montreal, we find ourselves, in a way, at the brighter end of the spectrum. Nature has invested us with mental faculties far above those of the millions inhabiting this area. That is why the master has gone out of his way to acquaint us with the reality of things in the spirit world. He has a special work for each one of us—and stop looking at me as if you don't believe me!"

Undoubtedly my face had shown my shock at what he had said so far. "Pardon me if I have offended in any way," I told him. "I do believe what you have said. But I have much to learn about the master's will—all I have witnessed here in your house of worship is so new and different from what I was brought up to believe."

"I didn't mean to snap at you, believe me," he replied, "and you have not offended me. It's just that at times I take things probably too seriously. I was not boasting in the way I talked about our people here in Montreal. The master explained that to me personally."

By then he had sat back down in his desk chair, lit a cigar, and was puffing away. "As for you and your friend Roland, it was revealed to me a year ago that I would meet you here in our house of worship, but I had forgotten all about it. And as I mentioned to you a while back, I was relaxing in a hotel suite in Chicago when a chief counselor appeared to me, refreshed my memory about you, and told me to get on the phone immediately to the person I had left in charge while I was away. He was about to wreck all the work that the spirits had done to put you in touch with us. I telephoned the man at once, and before I had time to say anything, he mentioned that George had asked for the permission to have you and your friend attend a praise session, and that he had refused him the privilege. Of course I informed him of the chief counselor's wishes. Then I called George to tell him that it would be a pleasure to have you with us. As you can see, the master thinks a lot of each one of us, so stop underestimating yourself."

After returning to my residence that evening, I experienced another almost sleepless night—the conversation with the priest kept running through my mind.

One particular evening my friend Roland had to work overtime at his job and didn't have opportunity to reach me by phone before I left for the meeting. While riding the streetcar home, he figured that if he went directly to the meeting place he probably wouldn't be too late. He decided to transfer at the intersection of Ste. Catherine Street and St. Laurent Boulevard and there telephone me at the house of worship. But he had left the phone number at home. If only he could remember its address he could then get the number from the information operator. So he pulled out a small note book he had in his pocket, and his pen, but try as he might he could not visualize the number he had seen so many times on the building. However, to his great surprise, as he whispered to himself, "I wish the spirits would help me," some invisible force moved the pen in his hand, writing not only the number of the house but the name of the street in beautiful script.

He felt quite delighted over his accomplishment until the operator told him that the phone number was unlisted.

About that same time George and I wondered what had happened to our friend. Then George got an idea. "Let's get Gerard the clairvoyant to locate Roland," he suggested.

After a few words of incantation, Gerard closed his eyes, placed his fingers on his temples, and said, "I see Roland having just entered the United Cigar Store at the corner of Ste. Catherine Street and St. Laurent Boulevard. Now he is talking to the telephone operator. He wants our phone number, but is being told that it is unlisted. I will, by the help of my familiar spirit, transfer a thought to him. Ah, he has it. He's dialing George; be ready to answer, as he will be asking for you."

George started toward the phone across the room. On the first ring someone picked up the receiver and, after saying

Hello, told George the call was for him.

When Roland arrived, he was delighted over his experience with the spirits. He showed us that beautiful writing on the paper and said, "I'm going to frame it. I have never seen such beautiful freehand writing in my life." Then turning to the priest, he asked, "I wonder, why didn't the spirit give me the phone number, as well as the address?"

"You did not ask the spirit for it," the man replied. "According to thy faith be it done unto thee. The experience you have had this evening is child's play in comparison with what the gods have in mind for you two gentlemen. But you have to exercise faith in the spirits and expect great things from them. What you need is to witness the spirits' power and intelligence at work a few times, then I believe you will be able to exercise a sufficient amount of faith so they will be able to aid you in greater ways."

Perhaps two or three weeks later when Roland and I entered that lovely residence, the Satanist priest greeted us and then added this announcement: "This evening you are going to witness a most interesting séance. An old acquaintance of mine is visiting your city. A prominent professor of history, historian in the fullest sense of the word, he has been affiliated with some of the leading French universities. His knowledge of fascinating details of history has made him outstanding in his field. Or I should say, the spirits have made him great. They have supplied him with many unknown facts of history. This evening he will—through a trance medium—uncover many details of Napoleon Bonaparte's war campaigns. He is at present having his devotions in the worship room. Meanwhile, let me explain what will take place."

Making ourselves comfortable, we attentively listened to the priest explain what should be a most fascinating séance. "A trance medium allows a spirit to enter his body, taking full control of his physical and mental faculties, and thus serves as a means for the spirits to better communicate with humans. In times past as many as six to 12 spirits have entered the trance medium's body at different times. One particular spirit may be knowledgeable about certain details on some points of history, but lack information on other aspects. Another one who was present and involved with the events that transpired at a particular time will replace him. The spirits are so precise that they can reproduce not only the words but the very tones and voice qualities of the persons they are quoting."

A few minutes later the priest left to check whether his friend had finished his devotions. Before long he returned to tell us that all those interested in witnessing the séance should go down to the worship room.

The priest introduced the visiting historian to the assembly, then asked for six volunteers to come forward. The spirits would choose one of them as their channel of communication for the evening. The six individuals stood before the priest, who invoked the gods to manifest their great powers to us by having the spirits who had directed and assisted Napoleon Bonaparte in his military campaigns reveal the details requested by the visiting historian. While the priest was performing a short ritual, a spirit entered the body of one of the men and began to talk. The voice had a Parisian French accent and a tone that commanded attention.

The spirit informed us that he was a chief counselor specializing in military matters and having jurisdiction over legions spirits. Since the subject was very complex, he would need two others of the remaining five men as spirit channels.

The two individuals kind of shivered a bit, their eyes closed, and the spirits suggested that they be addressed as Remi and Alphonse. The eyes of the man possessed by the chief counselor remained open but never moved, nor did his eyelids blink for a period of about 45 minutes.

The priest turned to the historian and said, "The gods are honoring your requests."

The visitor stood up with a clipboard and pen. First he

flattered the spirits, acknowledging that they had in times past given him information that made him one of the greatest in his field of learning. He conversed with the spirits for a few minutes, addressing them as Lord Remi, Lord Alphonse, and Lord Counselor. Then he asked question after question, and without hesitation the answers came.

At one point the interview referred to a certain conversation between Napoleon and one of his commanding officers. The chief counselor stated that it would be preferable for Alphonse and Remi to reproduce the dialogue that took place between the two men, for the sake of accuracy. The voices changed completely, as if two different individuals were talking.

Turning to George, I said, "This is fantastic!"

With a smile George replied, "If you think this impressive, wait till you hear the spirits reproduce the voices of people you knew who have been dead a long time. That really blows one's mind."

The historian, having had all his questions about Napoleon Bonaparte's war exploits answered, then informed the chief counselor that he needed additional information concerning a speech Mayor Camillien Houde made on the steps of the Montreal City Hall just before Canada entered World War II.

The chief counselor commented that he and his aides could not help him, since they had carried out all their activities in Europe, but that after their departure another counselor would take his place and supply what he wanted to know.

The bodies of the latter two men chosen as mediums shivered, their eyes opened, and in their own voices they asked how long they had been a part of the spirits' communications. As for the man occupied by the chief counselor, he shook a little, his eyes closed and opened again, and another spirit said, "It is my pleasure to assist you in revealing the unknown. I was present when Mayor Camillien Houde made his speech against the conscription of French Canadians into the armed forces. What would you like to know?"

The historian again stated his appreciation to the chief counselor for the continual guidance of the spirits in his life. "Due to the fact that no one was present who could make a shorthand account of Houde's speech, many different versions now circulate. Noble counselor, do you have any way of clearing up the matter for us?"

"I am glad to give you a word-for-word reproduction of Mr. Houde's speech."

What happened next amazed me beyond my ability to explain. I could hardly believe my ears. There it was—a voice I had heard on the radio probably hundreds of times over a number of years. Camillien Houde was a hotly controversial politician. He never hesitated to voice his opinions regarding anyone or anything.

In the late thirties Camillien was a hot topic for the French news media. His activities as mayor of Montreal constantly made the news. Radio stations recorded his speeches and comments and replayed them over and over, so his voice was easy to recognize. And now I heard that familiar voice again, but this time reproduced through the agency of a demon spirit. We listened to it for about 20 minutes.

Sometime ago I mentioned the experience to someone, and the individual said that it could have been the departed spirit, or soul, of Camillien giving the speech. However, at that time Camillien was well and alive. He did not die until the twelfth of September, 1958. Like the demon spirit had said, it was a reproduction of Mr. Houde's voice and words.

That evening as George drove us home he stated his belief that when a person dies, he or she is completely dead, and that when people claim to hold communication with the spirits of the dead, it is actually demon spirits impersonating their departed loved ones.

At that time I found his statement interesting, but did not give it a great deal of thought. George did not want to enlarge upon the subject, but instead mentioned that we should have the priest explain the matter to us when time would permit.

It so happened that the following Sunday evening we discussed the topic with the priest. He gave Roland and me an interesting account of demon spirits impersonating the dead, seeing it as an illustration of their cleverness in misleading humans. I got the impression that the man received great delight and satisfaction from recounting particular instances when the spirits had deceived great leaders.

The priest also alluded to three or four Biblical accounts, but since I had no knowledge of the Bible at the time, it did not impress me except when he mentioned as a masterpiece the experience of Saul, king of Israel, and the witch of Endor. He stated how the spirits had lead Saul to rule his life by listening to his feelings instead of the word of his God. And how they completely separated him from the Creator by causing him to commit a great abomination in the sight of the God of the Hebrews, and by that means actually accomplished his destruction. "No greater glory could our master bring to himself at that time in history than to lead the chief executive of the nation of Israel to bow himself before a demon spirit in the sight of all the inhabitants of the galaxies."

The man said that demonic spirits have worked through the centuries to convince people to accept the concept that human beings have an inherently immortal soul. He explained how spirits have taken great delight in impersonating dead loved ones or famous people—all in an attempt to persuade humanity that the human personality does not perish with the body.

Explaining why humans so easily accept the idea that they live on after death, he explained that a powerful change occurred in their intellect after Adam and Eve believed Satan's deception. "Distrust and unbelief toward the Creator became part of their nature," he said. "On the other hand, it became part of their mental fiber to respond to the voice of our master and his spirit associates."

The priest surprised my friend and me when he declared that a belief in life after death was a form of idolatry through necromancy. In fact, I nearly fell off my chair when he claimed that demonic spirits were continually defiling Christian churches by luring millions of Christians into a form of spirit worship that leads them into idolatry without their even realizing it.

"Contrary to popular belief," he continued, "necromancy does not just consist of conjuring up the spirits of the dead to communicate with them. Because human beings are totally mortal and do not possess an immortal soul, necromancy has inherent in it the idea that the dead actually enter a higher existence than they had when they were alive.

"According to the great master," the spiritualist priest explained, "people do not even have to seek help from the supposed spirits of the dead to find themselves enmeshed in necromancy. Belief in life after death in itself," he argued, "constitutes necromancy. It allows demonic spirits opportunity to impersonate the dead. When people believe their lies, it brings the master the respect and reverence due his great and glorious name. Also, it amuses and pleases the spirits that they have led people into idolatry."

As the priest went on exalting Satan and his wisdom, a great sadness filled me. My heart actually ached as I recalled the devotion of my parents and grandparents to the memory of their dead relatives. They had sacrificed and denied themselves much to set aside money to have masses celebrated to shorten the period of time those souls would have to spend in purgatory before they entered celestial bliss. When I realized that all that sacrifice had been in vain, the shock was almost as great as what I had felt when my mother died.

The following Sunday the spiritist priest gave a message he entitled "Christian Idolatry." It covered in much greater detail humanity's condition in death and explained how demonic spirits established and maintained the belief in purgatory to turn the minds of millions away from Christ. The speaker bragged about the advantage spirits have over the Creator when it comes to getting people to believe something.

"The Creator," the priest said, "cannot lie, and He does not sway peoples' feelings to get them to believe His word. On the contrary, He wants them to accept it because they trust Him to tell only the truth. On the other hand, spirits can lie, and take advantage of the fact that human beings listen to their feelings when it comes to deciding on the direction of their lives. Spirits make full use of that weakness by causing people to feel strongly about things the spirits want them to believe. They fill the human mind with erroneous thoughts. People naturally accept such ideas, and always will."

Satan's ability to deceive delighted the group of spirit worshipers, and when the speaker mentioned that he and his angels actually have millions of Christians involved in idolatry without their being aware of it, the audience broke out in applause and gave the man a standing ovation.

Again the priest boasted that the master had deceived the whole world with the belief of an immortal soul despite our age's scientific knowledge and enlightenment. Then something amazing happened that helped me to accept Christ and eventually to decide to join the Seventh-day Adventist Church. It was a question someone raised.

"What about the Adventists?" a person asked. "You can't consider them deceived like you say the rest of the world is. Why do they resist the great deception?"

"You are correct," the priest replied. "Adventists haven't been taken in by it. First, let me explain why I ignored them. There are so few of them when you consider the rest of the world's population that I didn't even think of mentioning them.

"Second, the reason that they haven't fallen for the deception is that they are not ordinary people. Permit me to explain. What I am going to say next may upset some of you, but it's true whether you like it or not.

"The fact that Adventists celebrate the biblical Sabbath of

Creation makes it impossible for spirits to deceive them. The Creator gives them special help and great spiritual insights. So in that sense they are not ordinary people."

That unique experience was instrumental in helping me make a decision for Christ. After accepting Jesus as my Lord and Saviour, I became an avid student of the Bible. As a former spiritist, I felt that I should thoroughly acquaint myself with the Word of God so that I could help others with the question of spiritism.

It deeply impressed me that the Bible declares that necromancy—the belief that human beings have a conscious existence after death that we can communicate with—is an abomination before God. I now realized that it is in fact a blasphemous form of idolatry that robs God of the glory due His holy name. We do that when we attribute to dead people faculties that belong only to the Creator, such as immortality. First Timothy 6:16 tells us that "[God] only hath immortality, dwelling in the light which no man can approach unto."

My encounter with spiritism has made me extremely aware that the belief in life after death is part of a list of nine activities that expose people to the world of supernatural spirits. Scripture calls all of them abominations.

Through Moses God told His people, "There shall not be found among you any one that maketh his son or his daughter to pass through the fire, or that useth divination, or an observer of times, or an enchanter, or a witch, or a charmer, or a consulter with familiar spirits, or a wizard, or a necromancer. For all that do these things are an abomination unto the Lord: and because of these abominations the Lord thy God doth drive them out from before thee" (Deut. 18:10-12).

God considered occult practices so dangerous that anyone in Israel found to be involved in them was to be stoned to death (see Lev. 20:26, 27).

As I really studied the Bible for the first time in my life, I was surprised to see how clearly the Lord states that the dead have no consciousness. In Ecclesiastes 9:5, 6, I read this stunning statement: "The living know that they shall die: but the dead know not any thing. . . . Also their love, and their hatred, and their envy, is now perished; neither have they any more a portion for ever in any thing that is done under the sun."

But the passages that impressed me the most occur in the book of Job: "Man that is born of a woman is of few days, and full of trouble. He cometh forth like a flower, and is cut down: he fleeth also as a shadow, and continueth not. . . . His sons come to honour, and he knoweth it not; and they are brought low, but he perceiveth it not of them" (Job 14:1-21).

Friendly Demonic Spirits

Several times I have used the term *friendly spirits.* Perhaps I should explain it further. The high priest of the spiritist group made it quite clear that Satan's armies of spirits are well regimented, and he assigns them activities according to their inherent abilities. The priest stated that fallen angels fall into three distinct groups.

He defined the friendly spirits as those of great intellect who have ability to impersonate the dead. In fact, one of their greatest delights is in appearing as the supposed spirits of departed loved ones. "As their specialty they operate in the religious world. They perpetuate the old errors that have worked so well for Satan for so long, and they are ever ready to introduce new ones as needed.

"The warriors," he said, "concentrate on sowing discord in families and misunderstanding between friends, relatives, and neighbors. Such spirits love to create friction between races and other segments of society. And those who have the best track record in dividing people and filling them with hatred and violence, Satan assigns the task of causing outright war among nations."

"The oppressors," the spiritist leader explained, "are a unique group in that they find delight only in producing misery and destruction among the human race. They suffered some kind of mental breakdown when our great master and his spirit associates were misunderstood and driven to this planet, and they have never recovered from the ordeal. Hating the Creator bitterly, they feel that the only way to get even with Him is to wreck the lives of those created in His image."

A few months later what he told Roland and me that night had a major role in my decision to break away from demon worship.

Chapter 6

Pressure for a Commitment

One particular evening, as Roland and I conversed with the Satanist priest, he mentioned that the time had come for both of us to begin exercising faith in the power of the spirits, since the master had instructed him that we should. "One of many gifts is yours to claim," he said, "if only you are willing to profess faith openly in the master."

It consisted of participating in a Satanist ritual in which we would state before the assembly that we recognized Satan as a great god, the supreme ruler of Planet Earth, willing to bestow wonderful gifts upon believers. We would then claim for ourselves such a gift as we desired. Finally we would seal our confession of faith by depositing a pinch of powdered incense over live coals on Satan's altar and genuflecting before it.

My friend did not hesitate at all. Even though I felt like giving the matter some thought before making a decision, Roland offered many reasons why that evening was the ideal time for me to take that important step in my life.

Although I am now ashamed to admit it, I gave in and went through with it. I asked for the gift of divination that I planned to use in the following way: In my sleep at night I would dream of the winning names and numbers of race horses at a particular track the next day; then I would go to a bookie and bet on them. That very first night I had such a dream. Most vividly I saw the winners at three race tracks on the coming Saturday, three days away.

On the day designated I proceeded to a bookie, and sure enough I spotted up on the board the names I had seen in the dream. Since I didn't have a great deal of money to play with, I placed a small amount on the first two races and won about $60. The third horse paid 21 to 1 because it was far from being a favorite. But realizing that the spirits had informed me correctly up to then, I figured that I should invest $20. The horse came in first, and I was the only person in the place to walk up to the cage to collect. I picked up the $420 cash, said Thank you, and left. Walking tall over my newly found good fortune, I headed down Ste. Catherine Street to one of the many fine men's shops and bought myself a tailor-made suit of clothes costing about $200.

Similar experiences took place on other Saturdays, and before long the owner of the bookie joint had his manager bring me into his office. He wanted to have a chat with me. After we had talked for a while, he realized that I didn't know much about horse racing.

"I'm amazed," he said, "over the fact that, having such little knowledge of the subject of horse racing, you pick the winners so well. Do you mind telling me who feeds you information?"

When he realized that he was getting nowhere with me he said, "You're too costly to have in my establishment. I would like you to leave and not come back. If you need the addresses of other bookies in Montreal, I'm willing to give you a list of them."

My sudden prosperity was nice to experience, but in reality it didn't make me truly happy. Somehow it brought no contentment. However Roland was having what he called the best time of his life as the spirits worked fantastically for him.

One particular evening something happened that really disturbed me.

After many persons had testified as to what the spirits had done for them, the priest suggested that we all go down to the worship room and have a praise session to the gods. "We will speak the language of heaven," he said. "It makes our master and the chief counselors very happy." His statement puzzled me, but I felt it was probably best not to ask how devil worshipers could speak the language of heaven.

Once seated in the worship room, everyone received a church hymnal (and I mean a Christian church hymnal). In fact, the priest mentioned three Christian denominations using that particular one. After he had performed a short ritual before the altar, he then told the assembly to turn to a particular hymn and sing along with him. The singing must have continued for 20 minutes. Not uttering a word, I sat almost in a state of shock.

Afterward, while we were returning upstairs, the priest came to me and said with a smile, "I noticed that you did not take part in our praise session to the gods. Do you mind telling me why?"

"I just couldn't profane those Christian hymns the way you people did. The fact that I don't like Someone is no reason why I should sing profanities against His name."

"I understand the way you feel, but after a while you will adjust. It's like the first time a person witnesses a live animal sacrifice. At first it shocks him, but after he witnesses it a couple of times he doesn't mind it anymore. By the way, we're planning to have you and Roland come with us to celebrate our high feast to the gods at a resort we have in the Laurentian Mountains. You see, November first is a very sacred day for our people. I will tell you more about it next week when we meet again."

While we were driving home that evening I asked George to clarify something I had observed during the praise session. After the people had sung for a while, some of them began to use a language other than French, yet the melody was still that of the Christian hymn.

He explained that the spirits took control of their minds, causing them to praise Satan and his chief counselors in spirit language, thus enabling humans to worship them in a more elevated form of adoration. Such a type of service, he explained, had a dual purpose. First, the fact that demon worshipers sang Christian hymns in itself derided the name of Christ. Second, when demon spirits assumed control of the minds of some of the singers so that they praised Satan and his chief counselors in spirit language to the melody of a Christian hymn, it constituted the highest form of blasphemy against the God of heaven, which pleased Satan exceedingly.

A number of references to live animal sacrifices had caught my attention, so I asked George to tell us about them. He explained that his people conducted them on November 1 at a specific place in the Laurentian Mountains, but that he preferred having the priest explain things to us. However, circumstances kept me from ever finding out.

Unknown to me at the time, the fallen angels became aware that God was working to bring me shortly to the place where I could hear of His great love for undeserving human beings, His plan of redemption, and His righteous character in dealing with humans. The spirits then determined to pressure me quickly into a deep commitment to demon worship. They wanted me to pass the point of no return, as I will explain shortly.

On a particular Wednesday evening when I entered our place of worship, I never expected that it would be for the last time. As I shook hands with those friendly individuals who had gone out of their way to make us feel part of their group in order to please the spirits, it would have been impossible for me to imagine that just 10 days later the same people would be vicious enemies planning my destruction, willing to spend a large sum of money to put out a contract on my life.

The testimonial session was most impressive, and after it ended, the priest had a short talk with my friend and me, telling us that the spirits were most anxious to benefit our lives in a very special way. On November 1, just two weeks away, if we would but make a definite commitment at an initiation service into their secret society, the spirits would then reveal to us their plans for our lives.

When I asked the priest why we had to go through the initiation ritual before they would tell us their plans for us, he explained that it was a matter of exercising faith in the spirits. Without faith, it was impossible to please their master, but pleasing him would in turn result in many benefits to ourselves.

"Gentlemen, please come with me. I would like to have you hear how the master rewards people."

We accompanied him to a room where earlier that evening, as I passed by the closed door, I had heard a fantastic clattering of typewriters. He knocked and someone responded, "Please come in." When we walked in, we found a man stuffing large brown envelopes with stacks of legal-size typewritten material.

"Julien, you have met these gentlemen before," the priest said. "But I doubt that they know your occupation and how the spirits bettered your life while you did good for others. So I brought them in to have them hear from you personally about your experience with the spirits once you were initiated into our society."

The man related to us that as a young attorney he saw himself destined to spending his life researching reference material or court cases handled by some large law firm. But good fortune came to him when, by the leading of the spirits, he became acquainted with demon worship. His life changed overnight.

After his initiation into the group, the spirits informed

him that they had a special assignment for him. He would help those who had committed crimes against society and were not receiving the legal advice they needed to avoid jail.

The spirits wanted him to venture out immediately into his own business. He would offer lawyers the unique service of preparing briefs for criminal court cases. The spirits would do most of the work.

They informed him that letters had gone to certain French lawyers throughout Canada, informing them he would supply attorneys with all needed materials to fight and win those types of court cases that in times past they had lost because they did not have time to prepare. In no time at all replies began coming in.

Next, the spirits told him that all he had to do was to work in the house of worship any Wednesday he needed their assistance. His efforts consisted in feeding paper into three typewriters until the spirits had set up each brief in its entirety.

On the table in front of him were the typewriters and about 50 piles of paper. They ranged anywhere between one-half inch in thickness to about three inches. He explained that all that material had been typed as fast as he could slip paper into the three typewriters. It contained the proper procedures to follow in court, case histories of similar cases tried in the past, etcetera.

When the priest asked him how the attorneys accepted his services, he declared that they were just delighted to use them because of the excellent results. To the priest's question of how much dollar value the work before him represented, Julien replied that it involved many thousands of dollars. As we started to leave he invited us to come in and observe the spirits at work whenever we found ourselves in the building and he was occupied with his project.

The priest repeated his request that we let them initiate us into their cult. My friend gave him a Yes answer, but I could not. "I'm sorry, but I cannot give you an answer immediately," I told him. "Next week at this time I will give you a definite answer."

Not realizing it, I shook hands with the Satanist priest for the last time, then left. After going to bed that night, I could not sleep. The thought of initiation into the satanic cult kept whirling through my mind. Should I go through with it or not?

The experiences of the past few months passed before me, and many unanswered questions regarding the forces of good and evil filled my mind. Even though I had discovered many amazing facts about the supernatural, I felt that it involved much more than just what I had seen. I realized that one could not completely trust demon spirits in their claims of what they declared to be God's unfair dealings toward them. Where could a person find truth? Certainly not in any of the Christian churches, I thought, or I would have heard of it by now.

In my perplexity I felt that somehow I needed help in making an intelligent decision, and an almost overwhelming sense of helplessness caused me to exclaim aloud, "If there is a God in heaven who cares for me, help me!" Shortly after speaking those words, I turned on my side and fell asleep. The next thing I knew my alarm clock rang. That Thursday morning I went to work, buried in my thoughts.

Shortly after I had met Roland and began to attend spiritualistic séances, I started on a job I had applied for some time previously. It meant my taking up a trade—that of embroidery for a firm specializing in that type of service to the dress manufacturing firms of Montreal.

During the time I was operating my embroidery machine, I mulled over and over the decision I had to make within a week. By Friday noon I had come to one—that I had no other choice than to go through with the initiation.

Chapter 7

From Demon Worship to Bible Study

At three o'clock in the afternoon a bell rang as usual to indicate the beginning of the 15-minute break period. As I passed by the office on my way out of the plant, Harry, one of the owners, asked me to stop in when I returned to work. He needed to talk to me.

When I later entered his office, he offered me a cigarette, then said, "Roger, I would like you to do me a favor. Undoubtedly you noticed my walking through the plant this morning with a young man, showing him our operation. Well, I have hired him to work here. He will begin next Monday morning."

"Boss, that's interesting, but what does it have to do with me?"

"Now listen carefully to what I'm going to tell you. It's very important to me. Since he has left I have not been able to think about anything else but a problem he has. The man is a Christian, but keeps the seventh-day Sabbath. Before taking the job, he mentioned that because of his religious convictions he would like to leave work at 3:30 p.m. on Fridays and make up the time on the other days of the week, so that in this way he could prepare for the observance of the Sabbath."

"Harry, I'm listening, but I'm not getting the point."

"I see that you're not acquainted with the fact that the Biblical Sabbath begins at sunset Friday evening and closes at sunset Saturday. Being Jewish, I understood exactly what he meant and told him we would work things out to his satisfaction. But I felt awkward about asking what religious denomination he belongs to.

"Here's what I'd like you to do for me. I will have Cyril work at the machine next to you, and as you two get acquainted with each other, find out the name of his church and the nature of his religious beliefs. Don't let on that I mentioned any of this to you. Be tactful, take your time, even if you have to wait a week or two before you bring up the subject. This really intrigues me—a christian keeping the Biblical Sabbath. I have never heard of such a thing before today."

Feeling an urgent need to set Harry right about the Sabbath and the correct day of the week to observe it, I said, "Don't you know that Sunday is the seventh day of the week? I learned that when I was a youngster in school. The nuns explained to us that God created the world in six days and rested on the seventh. But there has been an error made in the Gregorian calendar. In reality, Sunday should be on the calendar in the place where you see Saturday."

With a smile, Harry pulled open one of his desk drawers, picked up a dictionary, turned to the word *Saturday*, and asked me to read the definition. "'Saturday—the seventh and last day of the week.'" Then he explained that the Jews had never lost sight of the weekly cycle and that the Biblical Sabbath is in reality the seventh day of the week, or Saturday, as indicated by the calendar.

As for the Gregorian calendar, he stated that, while it did involve a correction of time, it did not affect or alter the weekly cycle in the least. It merely compensated for the fact that the calendar and the movement of the sun had gotten 10 days out of adjustment over a period of 1,600 years. He then suggested that I check a good encyclopedia and let him know my findings Sunday afternoon, since we were planning to play billiards together that day.

I admitted to the boss that I was not very knowledgeable when it came to religion, thanked him for an interesting fact of history, and returned to work, having agreed to get him the information he sought about Cyril's religious beliefs.

As I worked I couldn't think of anything except what Harry and I had talked about and couldn't wait until quitting time so I could go to the public library and do a little research. Then I thought, Why trouble myself over religion? What good will it do me? It's a waste of time. But again I felt a strong desire to look into the subject.

After work I went directly to the municipal library and in a few minutes had all the facts concerning the Gregorian calendar. I found that my boss was correct on the subject.

Pope Gregory XIII decreed that the day following Thursday, October 4, 1582, should be Friday, October 15, 1582, so as to bring the celebration of Easter back to the time fixed by the Council of Nicea. The Council had ruled that the church should observe Easter on the first Sunday after the first full moon occurring after the vernal equinox.

On Monday morning Harry introduced the new employee to all of us at the shop. "His name is Cyril Grosse, and he is an accomplished embroiderer. We welcome Cyril to our plant, knowing that his presence with us will add to the credibility of our firm."

He then walked Cyril to the work position next to mine, telling him that the new machine should be a pleasure for him to operate. Then turning to me he said, "Cyril, meet Roger. You two should become good friends in that you will be working on the same projects as time goes on. Roger, try to answer any questions Cyril may have about any particular work assignment. And if you fellows need help with anything, just call me."

About 45 minutes later I began experiencing some difficulty with my embroidery machine. Among other things it kept dropping stiches. That meant I had to undo some of the work and do it over again. After the machine malfunctioned a number of times my patience wore kind of thin, and I began to indulge in an old habit I then referred to as calling down the saints from heaven.

Eventually, I asked my boss to check the adjustments of my machine. He came over, reset the tension on the bobbins, and examined the machine for a number of things that could be causing my trouble, but it didn't help much.

At the 10:00 break, Cyril and I went outdoors for some fresh air and talked about my difficulties. I asked him whether he could think of anything I could do to solve my problem. He rubbed his chin a little, then said, "Seeing that you are asking my opinion, I believe there is. Roger, please take it easy on the Lord. I could hear your voice over the noise of the machines and I could tell it was not praying for help."

His answer to my question surprised me some, but he put it in such a way that he got his point across without upsetting me. I at the same time, saw an opportunity to find out what Harry wanted to know.

"Cyril, forgive me if I have said anything to offend you." I immediately replied. "I didn't mean to do so. By the way, I understand you're quite a religious man. Do you mind telling me what denomination you belong to?"

"I am a Seventh-day Adventist," he replied.

"Could you briefly describe what you believe in and why?"

Cyril explained that his church's name carries the reasons for its existence. "Seventh-day Adventists," he said, "are dedicated to proclaiming two great Bible fundamentals. First, the observance of the Seventh-day Sabbath as the memorial of Creation, calling all men to return to worshiping Him who made heaven, earth, the sea, and the fountains of water [Rev. 14:6, 7]. Second, Adventists look forward to the soon return of Jesus in fulfillment of His promise to resurrect the righteous dead and translate the living. Possessing immortalized bodies, they will travel through space with the Lord to God's own domain where He is now preparing homes for those who await that wondrous event."

By then our 15 minute break was almost over, and we headed back to work. I mentioned to Cyril that though I had no real interest in becoming a churchgoer, I would like to hear more about his religious convictions.

"Roger, it would be a pleasure for me to answer any questions you may have regarding my beliefs."

That particular October day was just beautiful, and a thought entered my mind. "Cyril, what do you say that you and I have lunch together outdoors? We could sit on the loading dock back of the building; and I would like you to tell me more about your religion."

"It sounds good to me."

Back in the shop, I found to my amazement that my machine now ran perfectly well.

I began to think about what I had just heard. Mankind's Creator calling people to remember Him as the Life-giver, and then, to show their appreciation through the observance of a memorial—very interesting, I thought. The return of Christ to earth, and the resurrection. People possessing immortalized bodies, traveling through space to a real heaven. The way Cyril talked about such things, he made everything sound as though it could be reality.

It turned out that the lunch period was the shortest I felt I had ever had. We had the same 60 minutes as always, but the way that the Word of God opened before me to solve the mysteries of my life, the hour seemed but 15 minutes.

"Cyril, what you have told me interests me greatly, but it has raised a number of questions in my mind," I said. "Could you answer some of them for me?"

"Certainly. Tell me what you have in mind." He made himself comfortable. "Maybe I can help."

To make sure that I had understood correctly, I began to review what he had said. "You mentioned the resurrection of the dead at Christ's return, and of people with immortalized bodies going to a real heaven. You stated that this would fulfill Jesus' promise to His disciples. Now tell me—what happens to people's immortal souls when they die, and what do they do between death and resurrection?"

Leaning back against the building, I took a big bite out of my sandwich and figured that he would spend a while struggling out of that one.

But right away he asked me a question. "Roger, would you be very disappointed if I told you that you do not have an immortal soul?"

"Not at all, but I know a lot of people who would. How do you explain that?"

"The actual word *immortal*," he said, "appears in the entire Bible only once [1 Tim. 1:17], and Scripture applies the term to God. Now, in all honesty, do you think that it would be right for you or me to claim that we have an immortal soul when the Bible declares that only God has immortality?" (chap. 6:15, 16).

When I heard his reply I almost dropped my sandwich. I had not expected that type of answer, but what he said made a lot of sense. "Do you mean to say," I continued, "that when a person dies he or she perishes completely? That he is no longer aware of anything?"

"Yes. In fact, the apostle Paul in his Epistle to the Romans encourages all Christians to seek immortality [chap. 2:7]. Obviously he would not suggest that we seek it if we already possessed it."

His reasoning made quite an impact upon my mind, especially since I had never heard a Christian talk like that before. I pumped him for more.

He explained that Jesus during his ministry on earth referred to death as a sleep. "Our friend Lazarus sleepeth; but I go, that I may awake him out of sleep. Then said his disciples, Lord, if he sleep, he shall do well. Howbeit Jesus spake of his death: but they thought that he had spoken of taking of rest in sleep. Then said Jesus unto them plainly, Lazarus is dead" (John 11:11-14).

Then he reinforced his position with 2 Timothy 1:10 which states that our Saviour Jesus Christ had abolished death and . . . brought life and immortality to light through the gospel.

When I asked him to clarify the statement, Cyril said that Satan and his demon spirits take great pleasure in confusing and misleading the human race. From the day that they caused our first parents to open the door of misery upon themselves and their descendants through disobedience, those evil spirits have followed carefully laid plans to lead mortals to focus their attention upon human philosophies and ideas. That way mankind would lose sight of God's great blessings that He had promised. "Sad to say, but the plans of the evil one have met with amazing success."

Now there's a man who understands the type of warfare carried on by his enemies, I thought to myself. Again I urged him to continue.

"The greatest blessing was to be fulfilled in the coming of the Messiah. Again, sad to say, the people of Israel, the ones who had received the oracles of God, became so confused about the Messiah that when He walked among them the majority of them rejected Him and one day shouted, 'Crucify him'!"

One of the most precious of God's promises had been the resurrection of the dead and hope of eternal life. In the days of the Apostles, however, the Sadducees—a learned class of the Jewish people—believed and taught the common people that there would be no resurrection (Acts 23:8). By contrast, many of the surrounding nations held the philosophy that when people died they entered upon a higher state of existence.

"We are to understand from 2 Timothy 1:10 that the Lord's teaching and great sacrifice on Calvary abolished death and overthrew all erroneous teachings on the subject. The gospel of Christ clearly indicates that eternal life and immortality will be granted, or given, the righteous at the resurrection of the just at Christ's second coming, and not before. And that when a person dies he or she has no knowledge of time, but experiences the sleep of death."

"Cyril, the Spirit of God has made it possible for you—I really mean all Seventh-day Adventists—to escape the ensnarement of the doctrine of the immortal soul. I am coming to the conclusion that it is the most powerful deception demon spirits have perpetrated upon us. Man, you have a lot to be thankful for."

I felt like telling him about my affiliation with the spirits, but figured that if I did, it could well cost me my life. So I asked one more question instead. "I hope you won't consider me some kind of pest, but could you tell me a little more about the return of Jesus, and the resurrection?"

My young shopmate summed up by quoting 1 Thessalonians 4:13, 14, 16-18. "I would not have you to be ignorant, brethren, concerning them which are asleep, that ye sorrow not, even as others which have no hope. For if we believe that Jesus died and rose again, even so them also which sleep in Jesus will God bring with him." " For the Lord himself shall descend from heaven with a shout, with the voice of the archangel, and with the trump of God: and the dead in Christ shall rise first: then we which are alive and remain shall be caught up together with them in the clouds, to meet the Lord in the air: and so shall we ever be with the Lord. Wherefore comfort one another with these words."

As Cyril and I walked back to our machines I commented "You have a most wonderful understanding of life. Anyone having this hope indeed possesses something of great value."

While I stitched designs with my embroidery machine that afternoon, my mind, unknown to anyone, became a battleground for a fierce conflict between God's Holy Spirit and Satan's unholy spirits. First I began to realize why demons so intensely hate the world's Redeemer. Also, I came to see why they have devised hundreds of theories to confuse and mislead human beings, especially the idea that humans are immortal. To back up their devilish doctrine, demons—as I had already discovered—appear to people and claim to be the spirits of departed loved ones.

For the first time in my life I discerned a God of love. At the same time I also became aware that I was a lost man. As I see it now, I experienced in some degree what those who will find themselves below the walls of the New Jerusalem, looking up at the redeemed, will feel. The ungodly will shriek, "It is too late."

Realizing that I was spiritually lost, I began to perspire profusely, even though it was moderately cool in the building. Opening my shirt collar, I rolled up my sleeves, but it did not help any. As I recall, I decided to go to the men's room. There I locked the door and, in the anguish of my soul, seized the toilet-tank cover to steady myself, since I became quite faint. Perspiration flowed down my face, heavy drops hitting the water in the bowl regularly.

It is too late, my mind kept screaming. Too late! I wanted to shout it at the top of my voice, but strangled back any sound. My hatred of God had now vanished, and my godless life loomed before me. At the same time I realized that I was a victim of satanic persecution.

Demon spirits now oppressed me with a sense of discouragement such as I had never before suffered—and have not since. I felt their presence physically to the extent that breathing became difficult, as though something was depriving me of oxygen.

In my helplessness I silently gasped, "May God have pity upon me." I had not meant it to be a prayer, but to my amazement, the suffocating condition left me immediately, and also the sense of discouragement.

After washing my face with cold water I returned to my machine. As I worked along, the thought entered my mind that perhaps the Life-giver had heard my cry and drove the evil spirits away. If so, why did He do it? I had hated God, had blasphemed Him. In no way could He ever forgive me. Yet no one but the God of heaven could have delivered me in the way I had just experienced.

Another idea flashed into my thoughts—that while I myself could not be forgiven and expect life eternal as Cyril had explained it to me, perhaps the Creator intended to use a worthless being such as myself to bring a blessing into the lives of those whom He loved and wanted to have in the earth made new.

I couldn't help feeling that God had worked things out so that I crossed paths with Cyril, who knew so much about eternal realities. Yes, it could be that the God of heaven had heard my plea for help a few days before when, lying on my bed, I had said, "If there is a God in heaven who cares for me, help me!"

He cares, yes, He cares. I almost shouted the words aloud, at the top of my voice, to every person in the shop, but I restrained myself. Now seeing that God did have concern for me, I decided I should ask Cyril to tell me more about what he had found in the Bible. If God had regard for me—a most undeserving individual—He must care for a lot of other people—good people, still unaware of what God desired for them.

Perhaps if I involved myself with the eternal well-being of others, God would rescue me from the power of demonic spirits, and I could live the rest of my life rejoicing in the thought that, even though I myself could not be saved, I could inform many of earth's inhabitants of the raging conflict behind the scenes, and thus lead them to make intelligent decisions for Christ.

After a while I began to feel great indignation over the fact that demons had mislead the human race. Then and there I determined that I had had it with them.

That day after work I told Cyril that I would like to walk with him to the streetcar and talk some more. While we strolled a long I inquired whether he would be willing to study the Bible with me. He replied that it would be a pleasure. Then he asked me a question. "Would you like to begin this coming weekend? Then we could have one or two Bible studies every week thereafter?"

"Cyril, for reasons that I can't tell you now, it's very important to me that we begin this evening. Should we meet at your place or mine?"

He invited me to his home for a 7:00 p.m. study. As we parted, he still looked surprised at my insistence that we start that night. Unknown to either one of us then, a week later to the day we would find ourselves having covered a series of 28 Bible studies.

Chapter 8

Monday Evening at Study

After he had introduced me to his wife, and we had chatted a few minutes, Cyril mentioned that he wanted to explain his association with the Seventh-day Adventist Church. Time had not permitted him to go into details on the matter at the shop. Actually he himself was not yet a member of the denomination, but he had been attending church regularly, and had made plans to be baptized on the coming Sabbath.

Unknown to his Adventist wife, for many months he had been reading all of the church publications that Cynthia had in the house, and in so doing had become an ardent Bible student. Also, he had obtained a deeper understanding of the Scriptures by studying them with Pastor L. W. Taylor, which had led to his decision to join the church.

Cyril suggested that Cynthia direct the studies we would have. I agreed that it was a good idea and bowed my head with my new friends while he prayed briefly.

His wife suggested that we use a new guide entitled *Twenty-eight Bible Studies for Busy People.* Each study consisted of about 15 to 20 questions pertaining to a particular topic. Each session would involve about one hour. The plan was acceptable to me, and we began with the first one, entitled "The Word of God."

It seemed that in no time at all we had covered it. What I learned about God's revelations to man delighted me. Lesson number two concerned the second chapter of the book of Daniel, examining the rise and fall of the great world empires, and the second coming of Christ to our earth. Cyril then suggested that we should set a time together to investigate the prophecies of Daniel. Immediately I asked whether we could have that study right then and there. They agreed, and we proceeded.

One verse above all others made a lasting impact upon my mind. "In the days of these kings shall the God of heaven set up a kingdom, which shall never be destroyed: and the kingdom shall not be left to other people, but it shall break in pieces and consume all these kingdoms, and it shall stand for ever." (chap. 2:44).

After reading it I wanted to know what else Daniel had learned about the establishment of Christ's kingdom upon earth. Cyril's wife directed my attention to chapter seven. "And the kingdom and dominion, and the greatness of the kingdom under the whole heaven, shall be given to the people of the saints of the most High, whose kingdom is an everlasting kingdom, and all dominions shall serve and obey him" (verse 27).

Cynthia mentioned that the words of Jesus in Matthew 5:5 would then be fulfilled: "Blessed are the meek: for they shall inherit the earth." Also I discovered that the people who will then inhabit the earth will be those resurrected and those translated at Christ's coming.

It seemed hardly anytime before we had completed the third study. Such things I had never heard before. They gripped my heart, and I wanted more. "What is the next study about?" I can't recall presently what its title was, but I do remember that it awakened in me a desire to hear what the Word of God had to say on that particular subject to the extent that I felt I must somehow talk them into one more that evening.

Lighting another cigarette and taking a couple of deep breaths, I commented that if Cyril would be kind enough to empty my ashtray, I could settle down for another hour. He emptied and courteously returned it to me. So I said, "Let's not lose any time so that you folks will not get to bed too late." They replied that they usually went to sleep about 11:00 p.m. "Great," I said, "it's just a few minutes past 9:00. We are doing well in our studies, so let's not waste any time."

I remember their reaction as if it were yesterday. Cynthia glanced at her husband with a large question mark in her eyes. He indicated that they should continue. Meanwhile I had nervously puffed on my last cigarette to the point that it was half gone. So I inquired whether they would mind if I lighted a cigar. Besides, it was my custom to reward myself whenever I felt I had accomplished something worthwhile. Studying the Bible with them, I believed, had been one of the most profitable things I had done in my life.

Without hesitation Cyril answered, "We like you to feel at home while you're in our house. Make yourself comfortable." That I did in the only way I knew how. The air in the room quickly turned blue from the smoke.

I have a firm conviction that the Spirit of God had gone before me, helping them to understand the powerful hold tobacco had on me, and to put up with the unpleasantness in order to acquaint me with Jesus.

Over the years I have thanked God many times for the way they handled the delicate situation. For seven consecutive days we studied the Bible four hours per evening. Not until we dealt with the topic of healthful living did I realize what tobacco was doing to me, and what they had put up with. And that subject did not come until almost at the end of the series.

When I asked them why they had tolerated my smoking, Cynthia explained, "We enjoyed your company, and when after the first evening you expressed the desire to return, Cyril and I decided that even if your smoking shortened our lives by a couple of years, we wouldn't mind if it meant your studying the Word of God and becoming a follower of Jesus."

Now, back to the fourth study of the evening. The Word of God was opening eternal realities to me, and wanting more of the same, I asked the topic of number four. "Could we have this fourth one? Then I will let you folks go to bed."

An expression of great surprise appeared on their faces. Then Cyril replied, "Why don't we plan for you to come back another evening this week, and we'll have it then."

"I hope that you will let me return tomorrow evening to have study number five. That is, if I'm still alive." Somehow I felt that demon spirits might do away with me. I did not tell them the way I really felt, but they sensed my urgency and agreed to cover that fourth study.

The evening when my friend Roland and I first visited the so called worship room of the gods, the priest had sworn us to secrecy concerning what we had seen and heard. We repeated part of the incantation after him and sealed the pact by depositing a pinch of powdered incense slowly above the flame of a black candle. The priest stressed that we must maintain complete silence on the outside to avoid the spirits' great displeasure.

Sometime later when we attended what demon worshipers like to call a praise session to the gods, the priest explained the great danger facing anyone who aroused the spirits' wrath. As an illustration he mentioned an individual who had allowed himself to be disloyal in what some would probably have regarded as of little importance. Even though he lived in what everyone considered a fire proof building, the spirits burned the place down with everything in it, including the turncoat and his wife. George told us that he had known the people.

Another time the spirits spent an hour terrorizing an unfaithful member in his home. They tossed everything in the house against the walls with great force, even shattering large pieces of furniture. Hospitalized in a state of shock after his neighbors found him in his home, the man almost lost his sanity.

With such experiences in the back of my mind, I naturally considered study time at a premium, which drove me to press for the fourth study. The boldness with which I ventured out in studying the Bible under such conditions was not the result of human effort. But, as I see it today, it directly resulted from having been fed the Word of God at work that day. God's Word is life. It has power to motivate a person even to the point of daring the displeasure of the prince of darkness. God had purposed that I should hear the great truths of His Holy Word, and it became reality. And in no way could demon spirits prevent that from taking place.

At the end of the fourth study we agreed to meet again at 7:00 the next evening. Before leaving, I suggested to Cyril that he read a couple of verses of Scripture and offer a short prayer. He opened the Bible to the Psalms. "'God is our refuge and strength, a very present help in trouble. Therefore will not we fear, though the earth be removed, and though the mountains be carried into the midst of the sea; though the waters thereof roar and be troubled, though the mountains shake with the swelling thereof'" (Ps. 46:1-3).

Just as I was about to depart, my hand on the door knob, I thought of asking Cynthia what studies were coming up. One of the lessons was entitled, "The State of the Dead."

As I said good night, I felt that I could hardly wait for the next study time to arrive. But in reality, waiting for the time to pass was not my main concern. While I rode the streetcar home I wondered whether I would still be alive by 7:00 p.m. Tuesday. I really expected a visit from the spirits that Monday night—against whose attacks I had in my own strength no method of defense. Yet I had no fear of dying. The Spirit of the Lord was blessing my life, undeserving though I was, for the sake of Jesus.

When I went to bed the words of Scripture that Cyril had read kept repeating themselves in my mind, and the next thing I knew, my alarm clock rang. Tuesday morning had arrived, and it was soon time to go to work. To this day the words of Psalm 46 still mean much to me, for they led me to look up to God, who is the fountain of life, the source of all power. The One who is able to wonderfully change the most hopeless, discouraging outlook, to deliver the helpless from the hand of the destroyer.

Chapter 9

Studying on Borrowed Time

Tuesday evening at 7:00 sharp I arrived at the Grosses' residence. The state, or condition, of the dead would be the focal point of our attention. I found the Bible quite clear on the subject, answering such questions as—

Do human beings possess immortality?

Can the dead praise the Lord?

Is the realm of the dead a potential source of knowledge?

The answer to the first question came loud and clear from the First Epistle to Timothy. Only God has immortality (chap. 6:15, 16)—or in other words, man is fully mortal.

"The dead praise not the Lord, neither any that go down into silence" (Ps. 115:17) answered the second question like a bolt of lightning. It shattered into a thousand pieces the religious teachings of my childhood.

The answer to question three began to reveal to me the love and justice of God in dealing with us poor mortals. We found it in the fourteenth chapter of Job: "Man that is born of a woman is of few days, and full of trouble. He cometh forth like a flower, and is cut down: He fleeth also as a shadow, and continueth not." "His sons come to honour, and he knoweth it not; and they are brought low, but he perceiveth it not of them" (verses 1, 2, 21).

After reading the passage I felt a great sense of relief. And I said to Cyril and Cynthia, "It's great to know that our departed loved ones are neither suffering in purgatory nor in heaven seeing the distresses of their relatives on earth, but all are sleeping in the grave till the resurrection morning."

The Holy Spirit then gave me to understand that death is the complete opposite of life, a state involving the complete extinction, or nonexistence, of life. Now I realized the total error of the concept that man has an immortal soul, especially after I read the record of Adam's creation given us in the second chapter of Genesis: "And the Lord God formed man of the dust of the ground, and breathed into his nostrils the breath of life; and man became a living soul" (verse 7). I understood clearly that God's breath of life is that agency by which He vivifies and sustains our physical frames. It causes the lungs to expand, the heart to beat, the blood to flow, the limbs to move. And whenever God withdraws it, life ceases.

By declaring in the Scriptures that man became a living soul—contrary to the popular belief that man received a soul—God loses all avenues for Satan and his demon spirits to mislead us by appearing and claiming to be the spirits of departed loved ones who have supposedly entered a higher state of existence.

At the conclusion of our study on man's state in death, a whole new perspective on God's character opened before me. I became deeply impressed with the thought that the Christian world has highly misrepresented Him.

For you to understand and appreciate what I experienced during that week, you must imagine that you never owned a Bible, much less studied one. Life offers no real joy in that no sooner do you find something to enjoy than there comes the thought that death could end it all tomorrow. You always face eternity, but an eternity of what? Other people do not know any more than you do. Then one day, in a most unexpected way, you meet someone who holds a Book written by the Life-giver Himself. All the unanswered questions that have troubled your mind over the years now receive an intelligent explanation—and more.

I found that through the doctrine of the resurrection the Bible opens the way whereby all men can gain immortality. "Behold, I shew you a mystery," Paul said. "We shall not all sleep, but we shall all be changed, in a moment, in the twinkling of an eye, at the last trump: for the trumpet shall sound, and the dead shall be raised incorruptible, and we shall be changed. For this corruptible must put on incorruption, and this mortal must put on immortality. So when this corruptible shall have put on incorruption, and this mortal shall have put on immortality, then shall be brought to pass the saying that is written, Death is swallowed up in victory. O death, where is thy sting? O grave, where is thy victory?" (1 Cor. 15:51-55).

Jesus, the Prince of life, when He appears at His second coming with the heavenly angels, will give immortality to those who have made Him their Lord. He will restore life to those who have lost it for Christ's sake. The resurrection is the great event to which holy writers looked forward as the object of their hope.

The apostle Paul, though he had suffered the loss of all things for Christ, still felt joy, setting his hope in the resurrection from the dead (Phil. 3:7, 8, 10, 11). He continuously directed his thoughts toward heaven: "Whence also we look for the Saviour, the Lord Jesus Christ: who shall change our vile body, that it may be fashioned like unto his glorious body" (verses 20, 21). I found it interesting also that when telling of his troubles in Asia, and of how he despaired even of life, he trusted in God, who will raise the dead (2 Cor. 1:8, 9). The apostle made no comment of his expecting to meet his

Lord at death, as taught by modern theology, but based his hope on the resurrection.

In searching the Holy Scriptures to find the time designated for the righteous to receive their reward, and the unrighteous their punishment, I discovered them to be not at death, but at the two resurrections. Jesus' words stunned me: "When thou makest a feast, call the poor, the maimed, the lame, the blind: and thou shalt be blessed; for they cannot recompense thee: for thou shalt be recompensed at the resurrection of the just (Luke 14:13, 14).

I found that Paul focused his attention on the Second Coming and his receiving personally from Jesus what he called a crown of righteousness. In the sunset of his life, a battle-worn soldier of the cross, his back carried the scars of wounds made by the lashes of five scourgings (2 Cor. 11:24). But the hope he held in the resurrection sustained him. Though realizing that he soon would face the sword of the executioner, Paul raised his voice in a message that would encourage generations of God's people, setting the time when all shall receive the reward of eternal life:

"I am now ready to be offered, and the time of my departure is at hand. I have fought a good fight, I have finished my course, I have kept the faith: henceforth there is laid up for me a crown of righteousness, which the Lord, the righteous judge, shall give me at that day: and not to me only, but unto all them also that love his appearing" (2 Tim. 4:6-8).

Throughout that entire study on the resurrection of the body, there lurked in the back of my mind the thought that if the New Testament writers believed that man has an immortal soul that goes to heaven at death, they would surely make mention of Christ's bringing it back with Him to reunite it with its former body. Nowhere did I find such an idea, but many texts of Scripture proved the opposite. For instance, in the fifteenth chapter of 1 Corinthians, where Paul speaks at length about the righteous dead and the resurrection, he states several times about the people's having fallen asleep and how Jesus will come and wake them up.

My last point of discovery—and one of the most impressive to my mind—on the subject of the resurrection appears in the Epistle to the Hebrew Christians. The eleventh chapter recounts the faith of God's people in various ages, and speaks of their trials and difficulties, of their courage, and of their hope in the resurrection and of eternal life, which sustained them even in the face of death.

"Others were tortured, not accepting deliverance; that they might obtain a better resurrection: and others had trial of cruel mockings and scourgings, yea, moreover of bonds and imprisonment: they were stoned, they were sawn asunder, were tempted, were slain with the sword: they wandered about in sheepskins and goatskins; being destitute, afflicted, tormented; (of whom the world was not worthy:) they wandered in deserts, and in mountains, and in dens and caves of the earth. And these all, having obtained a good report through faith, *received not the promise:* God having provided some better thing for us, that they without us should not be made perfect (verses 35-40)."

If only I could have this beautiful hope of the resurrection and eternal life to live for, I thought. Then something swept away that beautiful enthusiasm that had been building up in my mind. How foolish of me to think that God would ever forgive me of the hatred I had held so long against Him. No, it couldn't be. That hope of eternal life I had better put out of my mind. And there was my affiliation with the spirits. God could never forgive that. Forget it, Morneau, it's too late.

It happened that the passage Cynthia read to complete the study was Titus 2:12 and 13, which counsels all Christians to "live soberly, righteously, and godly, in this present world; looking for that blessed hope, and the glorious appearing of the great God and our Saviour Jesus Christ."

The passage prompted me to express to the Grosses my appreciation for their gracious willingness to study the Bible with me. I also mentioned that I wished I could live with the hope of seeing the glorious appearing of the Lord, but that my life had been such as to make that impossible.

"There is hope," Cynthia said. "We have a great High Priest, Christ the righteous, ministering in the Holy of Holies of the heavenly sanctuary in our behalf. He came and died on a cross on Calvary so that He could be our High Priest. Through Him alone we can find salvation."

If she knew of my involvement with the spirits, I thought to myself, she would not say that there is hope.

"There is hope for you," she continued, "sure there is. There is hope in Jesus for every one of us. There is hope as long as one is alive to claim help from Jesus. Let me show you."

She then turned to Hebrews 4:15, 16 and read, "We have not an high priest which cannot be touched with the feeling of our in firmities; but was in all points tempted like as we are, yet without sin. Let us therefore come boldly unto the throne of grace, that we may obtain mercy, and find grace to help in time of need."

I grabbed the Bible from her hands saying, "Let me see that." What prompted me to snatch it, I believe, was the fact that the Spirit of God was filling my mind with hope. During my days in the Canadian Merchant Navy, I once tossed a lifeline to a man who had fallen overboard. He seized that rope and hung on desperately. In like manner, in my lost condition I saw a hope and quickly reached for it.

Because of the lateness of the hour, I suggested that Cyril offer a few words of prayer, then I would leave for home. Also, I asked whether I could again study with them the next evening. They agreed, he offered prayer, and I departed.

While I was riding the streetcar—with its wheels squealing, the noise of doors opening and closing, people getting on and off, and the conductor shouting out the name of streets ahead—I stared through the window at the pavement. My thoughts were totally occupied with what Cynthia had said. Her words echoed in my mind: "There is hope for you, sure there is. There is hope in Jesus for very one of us. There is hope as long as one is alive to claim help from Jesus."

Then a voice seemed to whisper to my mind that there was hope for the hopeless, for the undeserving—even for spirit worshipers.

Thirty-two years later the Grosses met my wife and me in Toronto, Canada. They had moved to the United States shortly after my conversion experience, so we had not seen each other all that time. As we reminisced about those days of the autumn of 1946, Cyril made a statement that thrilled me, because in it I saw the merciful workings of the Spirit of God's love in my behalf.

"After several months marriage," he said, "I sat in on some Bible studies with Warren Taylor, the pastor of the English SDA church in Montreal. I had no problem believing anything Pastor Taylor said because all he did was quote the Bible. Then one evening he gave the lesson about the Sabbath. It carried me back to a day in Halifax when I had once asked my grandmother about the correct day for the Sabbath. But the study still did not fully convince me. That night, without telling anyone else, I prayed and asked God to help me believe in the Sabbath. I requested that He would grant me the ability to convince one person of it. Then I would take it as a sign that God wanted me to keep it.

"The following Monday I started to work on my job as usual. However, I had grown tired or restless and suddenly decided to quit. Having heard of a new factory that needed men with my particular talent, that evening I went for an interview and, to my surprise, got the job, plus a larger pay. Then I returned to my old place of employment and gave them the required two-week notice.

"At last the time came for me to start my new job. That Monday morning I sat down beside a worker who had two strange habits. First, he smoked like a locomotive. I was thankful that we could open the windows. His other habit was that whenever his machine failed to work, he would surprise me with unbelievable profanities. I had forgotten about my prayer to God, but God never forgets the prayer of His children. Little did I know that this young man who sat next to me would that day request—and even demand—Bible studies starting that night. I didn't know the serious problems that filled the life of Roger Morneau as he sat working at his machine that morning in Montreal, Canada."

That almost sleepless night of mine a few days before I met Cyril, and that one sentence prayer spoken in the early hours of the morning, the Life-giver had anticipated, and he had prepared to give me the right kind of help.

When Cyril talked to God about his need for encouragement in Sabbath observance, and of his desire to share it with someone, the Almighty said, "I have just the person for you." Then His Holy Spirit moved into action, prompting Cyril to want to change his job.

And when the pressure mounted on my mind to make the most important decision of my life, God was there to help. His Holy Spirit had worked out all the details to perfection. I am thinking mainly about my Jewish boss, Harry, and his obsession to discover what denomination Cyril belonged to, and his request for me to do him a favor and find that out for him.

The Bible studies we covered that Tuesday evening gave me a panoramic view of eternal realities. The Spirit of God blessed my mind with a clarity such as to eliminate the need to delve into deep theological research, which would have required a long period to assimilate. Because I found myself in a crisis situation, my time was not mine to use as I pleased. I knew that a confrontation with the spirits would likely take place before long.

I felt as though I was living on borrowed time.

Chapter 10

Day of Promises

You will remember that I had promised the Satanist priest that Wednesday I would tell him whether I would join the secret society or not. The spirits had vowed to benefit my life in a special way. But in two short days I had become acquainted with some of the great promises of the Word of God.

Thus Wednesday morning I went to work thinking about promises and what I should do about all of them. It was a mind-sobering day. I did a lot of thinking and little talking as a thousand-and-one thoughts raced through my mind. By 5:00 p.m. I decided to walk home instead of taking the street-car. Too tense to enjoy any food, I decided to skip dinner. I had to make a most unpleasant phone call to my friend Roland to let him know that for reasons that I could not explain then, I would not be able to attend the usual Wednesday evening praise session to the gods. And for him to tell the priest that I would get in touch with him before long.

As I was walking slowly north on Bleury Street I passed by various types of shops without paying attention to them. But for no reason that I can explain, I happened to glance at one window for a moment. After I had continued another 20 feet it dawned on me that I had seen a Bible. Retracing my steps, I looked again. Yes, a new Bible was in front of all the junk displayed there.

The name of the place was something like Sam's Pawnshop & Bargain Store. Just back of the Bible stood a small handmade sign that announced, "This Bible on special today. Come in for a real bargain."

Slowly I worked my way through the crowded store. The showcases were packed tight and placed in such a way that one could hardly figure out where to walk. Racks of men's suits filled part of the room, while guitars and all kinds of musical instruments hung from the ceiling. Signs and more signs everywhere proclaimed bargains and more bargains.

A little old man approached me and said, "May I help you?"

"I'm interested in the Bible you have in the display window. How much do you want for it?"

"Oh, the Bible. Let me get it for you."

"Sir, you don't have to get it. I just want to know the price, since I do not have much money on me." But he went after it anyway.

"You have enough for this Bible, I'm sure. I just placed it in the window about an hour ago. And I'm running a special on it ." He went right on talking, and I tried to be courteous because of his age. "If you want a good price on a Bible, never go to a Bible store. Always come to a place like this."

By then he had managed to slip through all his junk and return without having upset anything. He must have been an acrobat in his younger days, I thought. Placing it in my hands, he said, "It's a beautiful Bible, isn't it?"

"How much?" I persisted.

"You will not have to pay the high price you would have if you went to one of those Bible stores. You see, a Bible like this probably sells for about $15, maybe more. Let me show you why." He opened it to the New Testament, saying, "I don't know much about Bibles, but I know that one that has the red printing as you see here is the best."

Again I started to ask him how much he was asking, but he beat me to it. "I had set my mind on getting a pretty good price on this one, but the more I talk to you about it, the lower my price drops."

"That's great. Keep on talking until you get to one dollar and fifty cents, then I will reach into my pockeet and pay you for it."

"It's sold. Give me a dollar fifty."

I really had not meant it, and proceeded to explain to the man that I did not want to take advantage of him and would be happy to pay whatever he felt would be reasonable.

"No, I will not take a penny more. Once I state a price, that's what I sell for."

As I was giving him the money he said. "Of course, I won't wrap it up for you. At that price I can't afford the wrapping paper. You don't mind taking it this way, do you?

"Not at all," I replied, and proceeded out of the bargain store. As I was closing the door I stopped, then went back in. A thought popped into my mind.

"Anything wrong?" the little man asked.

"Sir, this has been one of the most unusual business transactions I have ever made. Would you tell me honestly why you sold me this the way you did? You sounded as though you wanted to get rid of it."

He looked me straight in the eyes. "Son, this is undoubtedly a stolen Bible. I took it in last week with other items a couple of guys sold me. Up to then, I was having a good month in sales, but as I was thinking an hour before you came in, business has been no good at all from the time I bought that Bible. I immediately placed the Bible on sale in the window. Take it, son, go home and read it, and God bless you."

Instantly I thought of Hebrews 4:15, 16. Saying Thank you, I left. Real joy entered my heart as I walked down the street with my new Bible under my arm. I hadn't felt like that since I was a youngster. It was as though a cloud of gloom had overshadowed me and it now blew away. In fact, I felt so good that my appetite came back. Passing a Jewish delicatessen, I decided to get myself a sandwich and eat it at home while reading my new Bible in the time I had before leaving to go to Cyril's place for more Bible studies .

Something then happened that intensified my interest in the book of Hebrews.

When I entered my apartment I became aware that it was later than I had realized. Quickly I placed the Bible on my rocking chair and turned around to raise the shade on a window. As I did so I knocked the chair with my elbow, which in turn caused the Bible to fall off. "Oh, no," I exclaimed, "my new stolen Bible on the floor!"

It had landed right side up, open to the seventh chapter of Hebrews. "But this man, because he continueth ever, hath an unchangeable priesthood. Wherefore he is able also to save them to the uttermost that come unto God by him, seeing he ever liveth to make intercession for them" (verses 24, 25). My gaze moved down farther, and I began reading again. "Now of the things which we have spoken this is the sum: We have such an high priest, who is set on the right hand of the throne of the Majesty in the heavens; a minister of the sanctuary, and of the true tabernacle, which the Lord pitched, and not man" (chap. 8:1, 2).

Through those verses I heard Jesus declaring Himself to be a living, loving, and mighty Redeemer, able to save completely those who come to God through Him. And that included His being able to control demons.

While I traveled to the Grosses, I read the entire Epistle to the Hebrews. On my way back home I went over it again. And when I arrived home I read it a third time.

It fascinated me. The book showed me that Christ's intercession in man's behalf in the heavenly sanctuary is as essential to his salvation as was His death upon the cross. This made a deep impression upon my mind.

I saw Jesus as one who loves the unlovable. As one who is able to make all things right. The Lord of glory, I realized, had allowed man to nail Him to a cross "that through death he might destroy him that had the power of death, that is, the devil" (chap. 2:14). My only hope, I now understood, was to place my trust in the merits of the blood of Him who can save all who come to Him.

Of the four Bible studies covered that Wednesday evening at Cyril's residence, one above all stands before my mind in importance. It was entitled "The Destiny of the Wicked."

By then the Bible had revealed to me the Life-giver as a God of love, a God who loved the world so much that He gave His Son that whoever believed in Him "should not perish, but have everlasting life" (John 3:16). Two additional scriptural declarations enforced that fact in a way that I would never forget. First, that God did not send the Son into the world to condemn it, but to save it (verse 17). Second, that God wants to save all men (1 Tim. 2:4). Thus I discovered that love prompts all of God's relationships toward humanity.

How would such a God, I wondered, deal with those who rejected His offer? Would He change into the opposite kind of being—that is, would God now find pleasure in endlessly torturing them as most Christians seemed to think? I was most eager to find out what the Bible had to say about it.

Our study first looked into the origin of evil, its author, and how God will deal with him when sin will have run its course. Isaiah states; "How art thou fallen from heaven, Lucifer, son of the morning!" (Isa. 14:12). Ezekiel 28:12-15 describes Lucifer's high intellect and the exalted position he once occupied in God's government: "Thus saith the Lord God; Thou sealest up the sum, full of wisdom, and perfect in beauty. Thou hast been in Eden the garden of God; every precious stone was thy covering. . . . Thou art the anointed cherub that covereth; and I have set thee so. . . . Thou wast perfect in thy ways from the day that thou wast created, till iniquity was found in thee."

Lucifer turned from admiring the beauty of God's character to self-admiration. Then that self-admiration turned into self-exaltation. "Thine heart was lifted up because of thy beauty, thou hast corrupted thy wisdom by reason of thy brightness" (verse 17). His self-interest multiplied itself manyfold, and the time came when he had decided on a course of action that he felt could place him in equality with God and above Christ.

The prophet Isaiah said: "Thou hast said in thine heart, I will ascend into heaven, I will exalt my throne above the stars of God: I will sit also upon the mount of the congregation, in the sides of the north: I will ascend above the heights of the clouds; I will be like the most High" (Isa. 14:13, 14).

Interesting as the Biblical allusions to Satan's rebellion are, the thing that captured my attention the most was what God will do with the fallen cherub after Satan and his fallen angels have manifested their true character before the universe.

Ezekiel declares that "I [God] will bring forth a fire from the midst of thee, it shall devour thee, and I will bring thee to ashes upon the earth in the sight of all them that behold thee. . . . Thou shalt be a terror, and never shalt thou be any more" (Eze . 28:18, 19). The Life-giver will bring the author of sin and death to an end. The devil will no longer exist.

After reading that passage of Scripture for the first time, I thought to myself, then said to the Grosses, "How could some christian theologians preach that Satan will have eternal life in a lake of fire when the Bible so plainly says the opposite?"

Mrs. Grosse explained that I should not be too surprised. One third of the angels, beings of great intellect, became so confused in heaven that they sided with Lucifer at the risk of eternal ruin (see Rev. 12:4, 9).

We then looked at what the Bible has to say about the eternal destiny of wicked human beings. Psalm 37:20 states that "the wicked shall perish, and the enemies of the Lord shall be as the fat of lambs: they shall consume; into smoke shall they consume away." The passage clearly indicates the extent of the destruction of those who will have rejected God's mercy and persisted in self-destruction.

My mind went back to my childhood. People living in the country then customarily made their own laundry soap. Usually my father did it during the cold winter months, when it was more comfortable to have a hot fire going. It required melting down large amounts of animal fat and boiling it for many long hours over a huge wood-burning stove in the barn.

My brother Edgar and I would amuse ourselves by dropping bits of animal fat on top of the roaring stove. We enjoyed seeing how fast the substance would consume and vanish.

So the Bible declares that, like fat in a fire, God will eradicate evildoers and all traces of sin from the face of our planet.

Finally we closed the study by reading and reflecting on a passage portraying the reward of the wicked. Malachi 4:1-3 says: "Behold, the day cometh, that shall burn as an oven; and all the proud, yea, and all that do wickedly, shall be stubble: and the day that cometh shall burn them up, saith the Lord of hosts, that it shall leave them neither root nor branch. . . . And ye shall tread down the wicked; for they shall be ashes under the soles of your feet in the day that I shall do this, saith the Lord of hosts."

Cyril stated that although the great monarch of the universe is a God of love, at the same time He is a God of justice. While the element of love controls His being, we must never forget that those who reject His love, His infinite sacrifice made in the death of His Son on Calvary, will have condemned themselves. They bear the guilt of rejecting the Spirit of grace.

"There will be a day," Cyril continued, "when God will execute the sentence of death that people will have brought upon themselves. It will be eternal death, 'for the wages of sin is death' (Rom. 6:23)."

I then understood that the doctrine of eternal torment preached from Christian pulpits has caused hundreds of thousands of people to thrust God out of their mind and life. Early in my life I too had fallen victim to its sophistry.

Also, I realized that in order for anyone to study the destiny of the wicked from God's Holy Word and get a correct understanding of it, one must begin with the fact that the law of love is the very foundation of His government. All of God's actions toward the people He has created originate from that premise. Thus it is impossible to believe in the doctrine of eternal torment. This particular Bible study served to remove from my heart all that had embittered me toward God.

Afterward Cyril explained that humanity's thousands of years of suffering are the direct result of Lucifer's actions in heaven at the beginning of his great rebellion. The high position he held in God's government gave great power to what he said and substance to the claims he made. Mystery shrouded his real objectives. The inhabitants of heaven could not visualize the end results of Lucifer's actions. Sin intruded its presence in every department of the divine government. Lucifer coveted the honor and power that were God's prerogative alone.

The angels of heaven and the inhabitants of the universe could not comprehend the nature and final consequences of sin. For the good of all, God had to permit enough time to pass to allow Lucifer and his associates, by their wicked deeds, to manifest the exceeding evil and malignity of sin. The inhabitants of the universe have watched humanity's distress with silent horror. The events they have observed have left an indelible impression on their mind.

Delighted by Cyril's description of the great spiritual conflict, I could have listened to him for hours, but he did not want to give me "spiritual indigestion" (his own words). After one more point, we would turn our attention to something else.

"When all traces of evil shall have been wiped off the face of this little planet," he said, "and Christ will have recreated it in beauty superior to what it possessed at its origin, then one pulse of harmony and happiness will beat throughout God's vast creation. What a wonderful age that will be."

The way Cyril and Cynthia opened before me the reality of the great spiritual struggle taking place between the forces of good and evil impressed me with the fact that the Holy Spirit of God was working—and had worked in powerful and wonderful ways over the years—to bring me to the very place where I found myself that evening.

I recall looking at my watch—the time was 9:20. Had not the Spirit of God intervened in my life as He did, I would have been conversing with demon worshipers. But now I enjoyed the blessed privilege of holding a Bible in my hands, and had definitely decided, with God's help, to break away from spirit worship. At that very moment the thought of it all caused a shiver to go up my spine. Goose pimples caused the hair to stand right up on my arms.

At the conclusion of the study on the destiny of the wicked, I mentioned to the Grosses that during the time I had been memorizing Catholic catechisms, I had encountered a number of expressions from Holy Scripture that books used to support the supposed never-ending punishment of the wicked. I could recall words such as "eternal fire," "everlasting punishment," "the smoke of their torment ascendeth up for ever and ever."

My hosts both agreed that the Bible does contain many such phrases, and that looking into their correct meaning would constitute a long study in itself, but a most worthwhile one. It turned out that we did have that interesting study three days later. As I will recount later, Pastor L. W. Taylor conducted it.

When I retired that night it was with the firm conviction that Cyril's God was indeed the Life-giver, the one to whom even demon spirits owed their existence. The fact that I had been able to study God's Holy Word without their interference testified to that.

But on Thursday night, when I returned from the Bible studies, I became aware that the spirits had visited my place. And when I reached home Friday, I became very conscious that the spirits were trying to tell me something.

Chapter 11

The Bible Sabbath

I had promised my boss that I would find out for him the reasons why Cyril observed the Bible Sabbath. To save space, I will skip the Bible studies we had on Thursday and Friday except for the one about the seventh-day Sabbath.

To begin with, Cyril stated that the Holy Scriptures speak of the Biblical Sabbath as being the seventh day of the week. "In fact, the fourth commandment of the Decalogue, spoken by God Himself, admonishes us to remember to observe the Sabbath day. The call to remember probably results from the fact that humans are inclined, because of their busy daily activities, to forget even some the important things of life."

We then turned to our Bibles and read the fourth commandment together: "'Remember the sabbath day, to keep it holy. Six days shalt thou labour, and do all thy work: but the seventh day is the sabbath of the Lord thy God: in it thou shalt not do any work, thou, nor thy son, nor thy daughter, thy manservant, nor thy maidservant, nor thy cattle, nor thy stranger that is within thy gates: for in six days the Lord made heaven and earth, the sea, and all that in them is, and rested the seventh day: wherefore the Lord blessed the sabbath day, and hallowed it'" (Ex. 20:8-11).

I was amazed to discover that the commandment to observe the day God had blessed was vastly different from the one in the Catholic catechism I had used. In fact, I immediately told the Grosses, "These are not the commandments that I memorized when I was a youngster." I went to the second verse of the chapter and began to read:

"I am the Lord thy God, which have brought thee out of the land of Egypt, out of the house of bondage. Thou shalt have no other gods before me. Thou shalt not make unto thee any graven image, or any likeness of any thing that is in heaven above, or that is in the earth beneath, or that is in the water under the earth: thou shalt not bow down thyself to them, nor serve them: for I the lord thy God am a jealous God . . ."

In fact, I read all the Ten Commandments and found them much more detailed than the catechism versions I had known. "I have a hard time believing that these are the commandments of God," I blurted out.

Cyril, using finesse and at the same time not minimizing their solemnity, said that they indeed were the commandments God had given to the Hebrews through Moses. Then he made a statement in the form of a question that blew the issue wide open before my mind. "Roger, I don't want to sound like a smart aleck, but could it be that the commandments you were acquainted with were those of some other god?"

Then it dawned on me, as in my mind I visualized the so-called worship room of the gods: The fallen cherub, the demon god, had in past centuries tampered with God's holy commandments to mislead the human family. I then pictured the inhabitants of the whole earth being deceived by the master artist of deception.

Returning to the study of the Bible Sabbath, I was struck by the great emphasis the Lord has placed on the seventh day of the week as one to honor. "And on the seventh day God ended his work which he had made; and he rested on the seventh day from all his work which he had made. And God blessed the seventh day, and sanctified it: because that in it he had rested from all his work which God created and made" (Gen. 2:2, 3).

One point that most vividly impressed my mind with the solemnity and sacredness the Creator has bestowed upon that day was the fact that for 40 years the Lord fed the Israelites on a daily basis except on the Sabbath. "Then said the Lord unto Moses, Behold, I will rain bread from heaven for you; and the people shall go out and gather a certain rate every day, that I may prove them, whether they will walk in my law, or no. And it shall come to pass, that on the sixth day they shall prepare that which they bring in; and it shall be twice as much as they gather daily." "Six days ye shall gather it; but on the seventh day, which is the sabbath, in it there shall be none" (Ex. 16:4, 5, 26).

I found it interesting to see how the Lord sought to acquaint the Hebrews with the sacredness of His Sabbath. And as we read that account of the manna experience, I couldn't help chuckling at the idea that some persisted in wondering whether God really meant what He said. "And it came to pass, that there went out some of the people on the seventh day for to gather, and they found none" (verse 27).

Having taken into account the writings of Moses and the prophets on the matter of the Bible Sabbath, we turned to the New Testament to discover how Jesus and the early disciples related to it. Speaking of Jesus, Luke states, "And he came to Nazareth, where he had been brought up: and, as his custom was, he went into the synagogue on the sabbath day" (Luke 4:16). Jesus declared to the Jewish people that He is Lord of the Sabbath (Mark 2:28).

The Lord of the Sabbath never intended that His Father's

holy law should ever be changed. For instance, in His sermon on the mount He left no uncertainty about the solid foundation upon which God's holy law rests: "Think not that I am come to destroy the law, or the prophets: I am not come to destroy, but to fulfill. For verily I say unto you, Till heaven and earth pass, one jot or one tittle shall in no wise pass from the law, till all be fulfilled" (Matt. 5:17, 18).

We also considered Biblical accounts of the early disciples and their observance of the Sabbath. After we had read so much in the Word of God about the observance of the Creation Sabbath, I asked Cyril whether he knew how Christians ever came to observe the first day of the week, or Sunday, as their day of rest.

He stated that the Roman Catholic Church claimed to have made the change in centuries past through the power God had bestowed upon her. "In fact, the church does not mind letting people know that she has changed the commandments of God."

The following Sunday I went to the municipal library of Montreal and did a little research in the religion department. Before long I came across a Catholic catechism dated back to 1930. It made the following comments on what it classified as the third commandment:

"Q. *What is the Third Commandment?*

"A. The third commandment is: Remember that thou keep holy the Sabbath day.

"Q. *Which is the Sabbath day?*

"A. Saturday is the Sabbath day.

"Q. *Why do we observe Sunday instead of Saturday?*

"A. We observe Sunday instead of Saturday because the Catholic Church transferred the solemnity from Saturday to Sunday.

"Q. *Why did the Catholic Church substitute Sunday for Saturday?*

"A. The Church substituted Sunday for Saturday, because

Christ rose from the dead on a Sunday, and the Holy Ghost descended upon the Apostles on a Sunday.

"Q. *By what authority did the Church substitute Sunday for Saturday?*

"A. The Church substituted Sunday for Saturday by the plentitude of that divine power which Jesus Christ bestowed upon her.

"Q. *What does the Third Commandment command?*

"A. The Third Commandment commands us to sanctify Sunday as the Lord's Day."

Impressed with my findings, I committed the section to memory. In the early fifties I acquired a copy of that very catechism, which I value highly.

While my first task was to bring back to my Jewish boss an explanation of Cyril's religious convictions, my next one was to find out how and where Christians became so involved with Sunday. That I researched in the months ahead, and made some most surprising discoveries.

In addition to my boss's interest in Cyril's Sabbath, and my own newly created inquisitiveness, someone else became aroused about the subject: demon spirits. On the evening of the coming Saturday when I returned home they attempted to reestablish contact with me (see Chapter 1).

On that Friday evening at the conclusion of the Sabbath study, the Grosses invited me to attend church with them the next day. Cyril explained that he would be baptized by immersion and become a member of the Seventh-day Adventist Church. We agreed that I would come to their residence and that from there we would proceed to church.

Chapter 12

A New Day and a New Life

Sabbath morning I arrived at the Grosses' residence and found that a couple of friends would also accompany them to church. After Cyril and Cynthia introduced me we chatted a bit, and as my custom was, I pulled out my cigarettes and offered them one, but they politely declined.

Then the thought entered my mind that it could very well be that Adventists don't smoke. A short while later when we were walking out of the house I asked Cyril about it. He told me that Adventists are quite health conscious, not as a means of obtaining favor with God, but in the interest of good health. Healthy people enjoy life more. He mentioned also that one of the Bible studies we would soon cover pertained to healthful living, and that it would present the benefits one can derive from abstaining from tobacco.

Immediately I assured him that I would not smoke while in the presence of church members that day. How in the world am I going to do it? I thought to myself. At the same time I told myself how fortunate I had been that the young people did not tell me at the beginning that I should not smoke. My addiction would surely have caused me to refuse to study with them.

At a later date, as I spoke with Cyril about the fact that tobacco had had such a hold on my life and that I would undoubtedly have refused to study with them if they had mentioned the subject, he said that after he and his wife had prayed about the matter, they had felt impressed to put up with it in order to acquaint me with Christ first.

At the time I did not realize that Cyril and Cynthia were attempting to reconcile Roger Morneau to the Life-giver. But the Spirit of God was leading them.

For instance, when I told him that Sabbath morning that I would not smoke in the presence of church members, he rejoiced that they were seeing their prayers answered. Before inviting me to go to church with them they had asked the Lord to bless my life in a special way. They asked for two miracles to take place.

First, that I should see and appreciate the sacredness of the Bible Sabbath. Should that happen, they would ask me to go to church with them. If I accepted their invitation it would be a sign that God was working a miracle of redemption. And second, that He would take away from me the craving for tobacco.

How wonderfully God answered their prayers. The thought of tobacco never entered my mind until about 7:00 that evening. Then for two hours my body went through an agony such as I had never experienced, leading me to conclude that I greatly needed a Saviour—one who could perform a miracle of love by removing Lord Nicotine, who had enthroned himself in every fiber of my body.

It was a beautiful day that Sabbath morning of October, 1946, in Montreal, Canada. Nature was beautifully alive, the air was crisp, and bright rays of sunshine piercing through the trees showered the earth with a thousand kisses of love.

The city seemed to be happier that day, and everywhere around us we saw evidence of a God of love watching over all. Having fresh in my mind a number of verses of Scripture on the Sabbath of Creation, I found that the day carried a new meaning for me.

I, a spiritist, walked with Sabbathkeepers to an Adventist church. My friends were not yet aware of the fact that I was slowly stepping out of the ranks of the fallen Lucifer, their most vicious enemy. It had been but a few days since I had my last contact with demons.

As we approached the church, I saw to my surprise that almost all the people on the sidewalks were making their way into the sanctuary. Someone pleasantly welcomed me to Sabbath school and gave me a church bulletin. Nearby I noticed a rack containing periodicals and tracts. Reaching over, I picked up a brochure. Once in the sanctuary, I felt impressed by a well-attended church.

After seating ourselves I began to read the tract while music played softly. It gave a detailed amount of information concerning the church's organizations and its various fields of activities.

The Sabbath school service began with a friendly welcome. The period preceding the study of God's Word was particularly inspiring and informative to a person visiting an Adventist church for the first time. I saw a people dedicated to being a blessing to their fellowmen.

The church devoted about 40 minutes to Bible study. Pastor L. W. Taylor taught the visitors' class. The lesson for that day focused on the life of Christ. Its central theme involved the concept that Jesus of Nazareth while on earth ruled His life by the principles of the Word of God, leaving us an example to follow. Pastor Taylor made a statement that I remember to this day: "If we follow our Lord's example there will come to us peace, contentment, and wisdom that the world can neither give nor take away."

His words could not have come at a better time. The Bible

studies of the past few days, culminating in the one on the Bible Sabbath, had led me to desire to turn my life over to Christ and to observe the seventh-day Sabbath.

The inspiring 11:00 worship hour culminated in a baptismal service. One of the candidates was my new friend, Cyril.

When he returned, I stated that—God willing—I would be there in church again next Sabbath. I also said that I would like to speak with Pastor Taylor if an opportunity arose.

On our way out of the sanctuary Cyril asked the minister whether it would be possible for him to give us some of his time that afternoon. He explained that I would be spending the day at his home. Pastor Taylor kindly offered to stop by instead of having us come to his parsonage office.

As we walked out of the church I couldn't help thanking the Grosses for their concern. At that moment it was not possible for them exactly to understand the blessings they had brought into my life. The Spirit of God had made them instrumental in bringing me to a spiritual oasis where Christ, who had spoken into existence all the autumn beauty that I beheld in the changing leaves of that beautiful October day, could regenerate me.

About 2:30 that afternoon Pastor Taylor arrived, and after we had visited for a while, the conversation turned to religious matters. I mentioned that we had been studying the Bible during the past week. He inquired about how much studying we had done and on what subjects.

After I enumerated some of the topics, I commented that we had had more than 20 Bible studies. I remember that moment as if it were yesterday. Pastor Taylor's eyes opened wide with amazement, then he asked whether he had heard correctly.

When assured that he heard right, he said, "Do you mind telling me what has prompted you to study so much?"

While I can't recall exactly what reason I gave, I do remember being surprised at his shock over how many Bible studies we had covered. I thought that anyone coming across Bible truth as I had would study the Scriptures in a similar manner.

Before I left for home that evening, the Grosses cleared things up for me. Some time earlier a number of the church members had expressed an interest in learning how to share their religious convictions with those not of their faith. They asked their minister if he would conduct some training classes.

Pastor Taylor had counseled them to use moderation in studying with those not previously acquainted with the Bible. He had stated that holding Bible studies once or twice a week should be the ideal, in that it gave a person time to understand and appreciate what he had covered. The pastor was right in suggesting a restrained, careful approach. But my case was an exception, and the Spirit of God lead the Grosses to do what was right for me.

I mentioned to Pastor Taylor the deep impression my visit to church that morning had made upon my mind. Then I inquired as to why other Protestant churches do not observe the Biblical Sabbath, since God has prescribed its observance as a means of obtaining a special blessing, one He has not placed on any other day of the week.

Pastor Taylor answered by first stating that the Seventh-day Adventist Church is in reality a prophetic church. As God called John the Baptist to speak to the people of his day—who had lost sight of the Messianic prophecies—that the Redeemer of mankind as among them, so He has raised up the Adventist Church to be a modern voice crying out in the wilderness.

Regarding the many Protestant churches not observing the Bible Sabbath, Taylor explained that God does not urge His ways upon people. On the contrary, He desires from all a service of love, homage that springs from an intelligent appreciation of His divine character. He takes no pleasure in forced allegiance, and for those reasons He grants freedom of choice to all so that they may respond to Him voluntarily.

After we talked awhile longer I realized that in no way could I keep secret my experience with spirit worship. My deep interest in religious matters made it obvious to Pastor Taylor that some powerful motivating factor lay behind it. As reluctant as I was to talk about my affiliation with demons, I felt that, having decided to break away from that evil power, the pastor could give me valuable guidance.

Once I had disclosed my activities as a spiritist, Pastor Taylor directed my attention to the Source of all life and power, Christ Jesus. He stated that "in him dwelleth all the fullness of the Godhead bodily. And ye are complete in him, which is the head of all principality and power" (Col. 2:9, 10). Then he cited a number of passages showing the Redeemer's power over Lucifer and the demons.

The discovery that all forces, including the fallen cherub and his associates, owe their very existence to Christ encouraged me, and helped me that very night during an encounter with the spirits.

Now I looked for an opportunity to ask him to explain some of the Biblical expressions used by those who preached the immortality of man. I did not have long to wait. When he asked me whether I had any additional questions, I briefly touched on a few of the discoveries I had made from the Word of God that week. I mentioned that our study had revealed to me that man is completely mortal, contrary to the popular belief that when a person dies, his or her immortal soul proceeds to its reward or punishment. The Bible declares that only God has immortality. We had read many Biblical passages setting forth the fact that the Lord would give immortality to the redeemed at the ressurection of the just. The unrighteous, not having immortality, would cease to exist once the punishment inflicted upon them has been carried out. But notwithstanding the fact that the Word of God clearly states that the ungodly will totally perish, some passages of Scripture do seem to indicate the opposite.

"As a youngster memorizing Catholic catechisms, I encountered expressions supposedly supporting ceaseless punishment of the wicked. I can recall such phrases as 'eternal fire,' 'everlasting punishment,' 'the smoke of their torment ascendeth up for ever and ever.' So, Pastor Taylor, I would appreciate it very much if you could clarify what seems to be a contradiction."

A sense of deep satisfaction came over me when he stated that there was no contradiction, but a lack of understanding on the part of those who cherish the doctrine of the immortal soul. Pastor Taylor explained that many persons misunderstand the meaning of the word *punishment*. They define it as conscious suffering and believe that when the senses no longer perceive any affliction, it ceases to be punishment. But when we look into human penalties, we find that we estimate a punishment by the loss involved, not merely by the amount of pain inflicted.

"For instance, why is the sentence of death recognized as the greatest punishment? It is not because the pain involved is more intense, for some forms of torture such as whipping produce more pain than decapitation or hanging. But we consider it as the greatest punishment because it is the most lasting. It deprives its victim at once of all the relations and blessings of life, and we estimate its length by the life the person would have enjoyed. So it is," he said, "when the death from which there is to be no release is administered, that is to say, no resurrection. That punishment is everlasting, or eternal. The second death deprives the sinner of the bright and ceaseless years of eternity. And just as the life of the redeemed is everlasting, so is the loss, or the punishment, of the wicked."

"Pastor," I said, "I like your sensible way of treating the subject. I don't wish to impose upon your kindness, but would you please explain it further? It's something that has bothered me for a long time."

"In Scripture," he continued, "the term *everlasting* and

the word *eternal* as they are associated with other words such as *fire* and *punishment* simply denote the results produced by the fire, or the punishment. They do not indicate the time span of the process of burning and punishing."

All ears, I sat on the edge of my chair. Excitedly I waited for the pastor to reduce another one of my childhood fears to vapor.

"Anything wrong?" Taylor suddenly asked.

"No, not at all. I'm just changing my sitting position a little. Please continue."

"Let me give you three short examples," the pastor resumed. "In Hebrews 5:9 we read of *eternal salvation*, that is, a salvation that is eternal or everlasting in its results—not a salvation forever going on but never accomplished.

"Hebrews 6:2 speaks of *eternal judgment*. Again, not a judgment eternally going forward, but one that, having once passed upon all men, is irreversible in its decision and eternal in its effects.

"And last, Hebrews 9:12 talks of *eternal redemption*. Not a redemption through which we are eternally approaching a redeemed state that we never reach, but one that releases us for all eternity from the power of sin and death."

Taylor said that when the Bible mentions eternal fire, it is referring to a fire that produces eternal, or everlasting, results.

"We are told in Jude 7 that the cities of Sodom and Gomorrha suffer 'the vengeance of eternal fire.' The apostle Peter tells us that God turned 'the cities of Sodom and Gomorrha into ashes . . ., making them an ensample unto those that after should live ungodly'" (2 Peter 2:6).

The way the Bible explains itself delighted me. I had never heard anyone discuss the subject so fluently and knowledgeably. Pastor Taylor backed up every word by sound Biblical references and left no doubt of God's goodness and love for those created in His image.

However, one expression still remained deeply rooted in

the back of my mind, planted by the religious instruction I had received when a youngster. For a moment I felt reluctant to bring it up. I assumed that he could not possibly have an explanation for it. Then I thought that if he did have one it would for all times establish in my mind the fact that the Lord is, in the fullest sense of the word, a God of love.

"Pastor, what does Scripture mean when it says, 'The smoke of their torment ascendeth up for ever and ever.'"? (Rev. 14:11). I sat back in the solid comfort of that overstuffed living room chair and eagerly awaited his reply.

Pastor Taylor explained that the Holy Scriptures apply the terms *everlasting* and *for ever* to things that endure either for a long time or for an indefinite period of time. For example, the Bible uses *everlasting* or *for ever* to refer to the Jewish priesthood, the Mosaic ordinances, the possession of the land of Canaan, the hills and mountains, the earth, and the time of service to be rendered by a slave.

"Either term denotes a duration or continuation, of time, its length determined by the nature of the objects to which it is applied. When referring to things that we know from other declarations of Scripture to have no end, it signifies an eternity of being. But when applied to something that will cease, it is correspondingly limited in its meaning."

He illustrated the point with a few verses of Scripture. Exodus 21:2-6 states that if during the Mosaic dispensation a Hebrew bought a servant, in the seventh year of slavery the servant could go free. But in a case in which a servant did not wish to leave his master, that slave could relinquish his rights to freedom through a specific ritual. The master would bring his servant before the community judges. In their presence he would have the slave stand by a door post, then bore his ear through with an awl. The slave would then "serve him for ever." In this case the term *for ever* could mean a duration of time anywhere from one day to many years, depending on how long the individual lived.

Pastor Taylor cited another interesting use of the term *for ever* found in Psalm 21:1-4. King David felt a thankfulness to God for the many times the Lord had spared his life. He exclaimed to the Lord, "The king shall joy in thy strength, Lord; and in thy salvation how greatly shall he rejoice! . . . He asked life of thee, and thou gavest it him, even length of days for ever and ever." David lived to be quite old, so the term *for ever and ever* here probably represented a duration of many years.

Having given me a couple of Biblical examples showing how limited *for ever* can be when applied to something transitory, Pastor Taylor then used Bible references where the term signifies an eternity of being.

The second chapter of the book of Daniel recounts the prophet's interpretation of Nebuchadnezzar's dream of the great image. Verse 44 announces that "In the days of these kings shall the God of heaven set up a kingdom, which shall never be destroyed . . ., and it shall stand for ever." Chapter 7 declares that "the saints . . . shall . . . possess the kingdom for ever, even for ever and ever" (verse 18).

Just as Scripture plainly assures us that Christ's kingdom, once established upon earth, shall be an everlasting kingdom, and that the existence of the righteous will be eternal or never ending, in like manner the Bible instructs us that the existence of the wicked will cease in the second death, which will take place in the lake of fire (Rev. 21:8).

During that Bible study a mountain of darkness and error rolled away and vanished. So-called mysteries that had perplexed the mind of my Catholic parents in their efforts to associate the character of a God of love with the doctrine of eternal torment melted away as ice would under a tropical sun. I had gained assurance that the Word of God does not contradict itself.

Suddenly about 7:00 p.m. I had an intense craving for a cigarette. To my amazement I realized that I had not smoked all day, and had not even thought about it. I figured the reason was that my mind had been preoccupied with the religious experiences of the day. In light of that, I concluded that I could put tobacco from my mind—and my lungs—if I kept busy with good things.

So our discussion of spiritual things continued. I brought up questions that had long perplexed me. The fact that the pastor had a Biblical answer for everything greatly impressed me.

But my problem intensified. I wanted a cigarette in the worst way. The saliva in my mouth thickened to the point that it became difficult for me to talk. The nostrils of my nose began to burn in the manner I usually experienced when coming down with a cold. After a while I became restless, changing my position often. Finally I developed a headache, something I seldom had. It ached all the way down the back of my neck.

At my insistence Pastor Taylor discussed religious topics with us until about 9:00 that evening. After his departure, the first thing I did was to light a cigarette, and I smoked without stop for about an hour. To my great surprise, all my physical distresses went away.

Before I left that evening, the Grosses covered with me the Bible study on healthful living, which touched upon the subject of tobacco. It made me aware that a health-destroying habit had enslaved me. Immediately I determined to give it up, realizing that I would have to go through an awful struggle to do it—unless the Lord of the Sabbath, the one who had taken away the desire for a cigarette for so many hours that day, would be willing to free me from it on a permanent basis.

A short while later I thanked my friends and left for home. On the streetcar I kept reviewing in my mind the events of the day, especially my episode with tobacco, and realized that I had more than one powerful enemy. At the same time I came up with a plan that I was sure would end my tobacco problem.

Pastor Taylor had stressed the great redeeming power in

the merits of the blood Christ shed on Calvary. In fact, he led me to see and understand that we can overcome the fallen cherub and his associates only through that power, as stated in Revelation 12:11: "And they overcame him by the blood of the Lamb."

I arrived home that evening about 11:30. Stuck to my door was a note to call my friend Roland no matter how late it was. It will have to wait a while, I thought. When I entered the place, I noticed that the spirits had been restless. Most everything in the apartment was out of place. Because I had become accustomed to dealing with the unusual, it did not trouble me.

First I took the three cartons of cigarettes I had in my closet and set them on a table. Then I opened my Bible to the twenty-seventh chapter of Matthew and read from verses 24-54 about the crucifixion. After placing the open Bible on the cartons of cigarettes, I knelt by the table and began to converse with my great High Priest about my problems. Thanking Him for blessing my life even when I was an open enemy of His, blaspheming His name, I confessed my sins and acknowledged the evil of my heart.

Pastor Taylor had made me aware of the fact that Jesus Christ ministers in the heavenly sanctuary for those in trouble, and that He specializes in hopeless cases. Realizing I was a real hopeless case for Him to work on, I grasped the hope inherent in Taylor's words. I struggled with enemies far too clever and powerful for me.

Thanking the Lord for encouraging me, I acknowledged the fact that the power of His love had held back demon spirits. And because of this, I wanted to turn my life over to Him, to serve Him as He saw fit. Then I would delight myself in the Lord by remembering His Sabbath day. Pointing to the cartons of cigarettes, I said, "Lord Jesus, please deliver me from this powerful enemy. Break the hold it has upon me, as You have already manifested Your ability to do so earlier this day. Remove that insatiable desire."

After talking with the Lord some more, I thanked Him for having heard me and again for His blessing my life. Then I rose from my knees, took the cigarettes to the bathroom, opened every package, tore them up, and flushed them down the drain. From that time on I never touched a cigarette, and never had the desire to do so. In a wonderful way Jesus performed a miracle of love.

(See the first chapter for an account of what took place next that Saturday night.)

Chapter 13

Episode of Death

Sunday morning I woke up to a new way of life. Instead of reaching for a pack of cigarettes on the night table—which had become a deeply established habit—I realized that I had no desire for one.

A surge of happiness filled me at the thought that I had a powerful new Friend in the person of Jesus Christ. I remembered the mighty way in which the Spirit of God had blessed my mind and sustained me during my episode with the spirits but a few hours before.

Realizing my human frailty, I asked the Lord to strengthen me for the conflict ahead. In the past the influence of others had led me to make bad decisions. Many times I had given in to the suggestions of my friend Roland. He had gradually led me into spirit worship.

During the next few minutes I prayed without uttering a word. Having learned that demons cannot intercept a silent prayer, I wanted to be one step ahead of my enemies. It gave me great satisfaction to keep them guessing. And I felt honored in the fact that I, an undeserving human being, could converse with the mightiest Being in the universe, and that demons could not eavesdrop.

I told the Lord that I didn't know where to begin in explaining to my friend Roland about eternal realities. Probably he wouldn't be willing to listen because he wouldn't want to offend the spirits. Above all, how was I to withstand the pressures to come?

A few seconds I paused in my thoughts, and as I did, a passage from the first chapter of the Gospel of John came to mind: "He came unto his own, and his own received him not. But as many as received him, to them gave he power to become the sons of God, even to them that believe on his name" (verses 11, 12). I then felt that the Spirit of God would carry me through my encounters victoriously.

On my night table lay my Bible. Reaching over to it, I began to shuffle the pages with the one hand, then opened it without paying any attention. On those two open pages of Scripture rested the power that would literally save my life.

A short while later I decided to get up. Picking up the Bible, I began to read where it had opened, the thirty-seventh chapter of Isaiah.

It told of a king by the name of Hezekiah, who had received a distressing letter from an invading tyrant, Sennacherib, who thought a great deal of himself. Impressed with the way the Lord handled the situation, I received additional confidence that I really didn't have to worry about what lay ahead. While I couldn't help being concerned, worry I should not.

At the time agreed upon, Roland arrived. "You look worn out, man. Are you sick?" I asked when I saw him.

"Morneau, you have almost shocked the life out of both George and me. We can't believe it—that you would be so unkind and so unappreciative of what George has done to benefit us that you would turn around and insult the master by refusing the wealth he has prepared for you."

"When did you hear about that?"

"At 5:30 this morning. George phoned me after a chief counselor told him about your stupid decision. He asked me to talk some sense into your head or you're going to lose it."

"I see how I must have upset that chief counselor quite a lot by throwing him out the way I did."

"What? Did I hear you say that you threw a chief counselor out? I don't get you."

"You heard correctly. About 4:00 this morning I had a conversation with a chief counselor, and when he became nasty I had the Spirit of God throw him out. He left his mark on the wall when he slammed the door open against it." I pointed to the indentation made by the doorknob.

"You—you, Roger Morneau, had a conversation with a spirit counselor? Do you know that some of our members have been worshiping and conjuring spirits for many years and haven't had the privilege of conversing with a chief counselor? And you have been dealing with the spirits but a short while, yet you are accorded that great honor. This shows you how much the master thinks of you."

His face glowed with excitement as he exclaimed, "You and I have a fantastic future awaiting us. Now forget that bit about christianity, and let's go and see the high priest. He will get you back in favor with the spirits again, and all will be well. The priest understands—he doesn't hold anything against you for looking into religion. In fact, he likes you and understands you. Said he realizes that you're an adventurer by nature. The priest recognizes that it's natural for you to search out a better way for yourself.

"The only thing he feels bad about is that if you were going to look into religion, why didn't you choose some other denomination instead of those Sabbath people—the very people the master hates most on the face of the earth.

"Man, you don't understand how much you've upset the gods. But I have the high priest's assurance that all will be well if you come with me now to see him at his office. He's there waiting for us. So, what do you say that we go right now, old buddy?"

When he pulled out his pack of cigarettes and offered me one, I declined, adding that I did not smoke anymore. Surprised, Roland commented, "Morneau, you're a changed person. I could tell the moment I walked in here. To be honest with you, I feel uncomfortable in your presence. You may find what I'm going to say kind of foolish, maybe even stupid—but I feel out of place here with you and wish I were somewhere else."

As he spoke I realized that Christ was fulfilling the words of the apostle John in my life: "He came unto his own, and his own received him not. But as many as received him to them gave he power to become the sons of God, even to them that believe on his name." I felt that the glorious majesty of the Lord Jesus reflecting upon me created an *invisible* atmosphere of power and majesty unconsciously breathed in by my friend, causing him to react the way he did.

"What you're feeling in my presence results from the fact that the Spirit with me is more powerful than the spirit with you.

"And as for your statement that I'm a changed person, you are correct. I will never again be the Roger Morneau you previously knew. In one short week I have acquired knowledge worth more to me than all the gold and silver the earth contains. That is the reason why I cannot accept the wealth offered me by the spirits. If I did, I would be cheating myself.

"Don't get me wrong. I realize that the spirits' offer is a generous one, but it lacks a most important element that should accompany it. *Life.* Life in a measure sufficient to make that wealth worth possessing.

"I have been offered a better deal. All the gold I want, plus unlimited life."

Then I proceeded to set before him the glories of eternal reality. Though I lacked the capacity to document them with

Biblical passages as the Grosses had, yet the Spirit of God held my friend spellbound for about 45 minutes.

During that time I covered those points that I considered vital. At one point when I paused for some kind of response, all he would say was "Now I understand." But he never asked any questions or made any other comment. So I continued.

"I can see that you don't intend to come with me to see the high priest," he said finally. "But you and I have to. You need to face reality again. All the wonderful things you have spoken about are not for you or me, so forget them. First, I don't want to wait for the good life—I want it now. As for you, Morneau, you have no choice in the matter. Maybe you think you have, but you don' t. You're just kidding yourself.

"Face it, Morneau, you're not your own master. I wish you were, but you're not. The spirits own you in your entirety, and the sooner you acknowledge that, the better off you'll be."

Extremely agitated, he projected an air of impending doom. He began pacing the floor, wringing his hands. "I'm on a most difficult assignment. What I'm about to say to you I'd rather tell an enemy instead of a longtime friend."

By then he was perspiring profusely although it wasn't warm in the room. "Morneau, your days are numbered—along with those of the young couple responsible for leading you away from the master. However, I must tell you that you can stop the plan of destruction the spirits have initiated, by coming with me to see the high priest right now. He will restore you to their favor, and all will be well. This way no one gets hurt."

He had to pause for a couple of seconds to use his handkerchief. Perspiration flowed down his face.

"One thing in particular the high priest wants you to realize—no one has ever gotten out of our secret society alive. The spirits brought you and me into it, and we're to be in subjection to them, not they to us. Let me explain.

"Up to now you and I have assumed that our meeting with George and his invitation for us to go to that restaurant was purely accidental. Wrong. The night before, a spirit appeared to him during the sacred hour and ordered him to go with his wife to that particular séance. The spirit told him that he would be meeting us, that we had served in the merchant navy, etcetera. He explained to George in detail what to say and what to do. The spirits had worked it out even to the point of his wife's being involved in conversing with the spirit medium to the extent that she would let George go home by himself, and have the Belangers drive her home later.

"So, friend, let's get going. Time is running out."

By then he had his hand on the doorknob, expecting me to follow. Pointing to a chair, I suggested that he sit down for a few minutes while I explained why I would not go to see the high priest. He refused, stating that he couldn't stand the atmosphere of the place any longer. A supernatural presence foreign to him made it impossible for him to sit and relax.

I commented that the presence of the Holy Spirit was assisting me in answer to my request for help earlier that morning. Urging my friend to break away from the demons and affiliate himself with the superior power of God, I assured him that he could safely make the transition. Then I felt impressed to go one step farther and invite the whole group of demon worshiping friends to follow me. Again I stated that I could guarantee that no danger would come to them.

"You guys like attention and respect," I said. "I'll tell you what I'll do—I'll call my pastor and reserve seats in our sanctuary for the coming Sabbath services. Choice seats, on both sides of the center aisle. I'll reserve 100 places, enough to make sure that everyone will be well seated."

"Don't go through the trouble," he replied. "I'm satisfied where I am now."

Again he had to pause to wipe off the heavy perspiration running down his face. "And I know the other fellows feel the same as I do."

"Well, I felt like offering to all of you the benefits of eternal life so that no one be left out." Then I changed the subject and returned to his ultimatum.

"You're telling me that my days are numbered, along with those of my new friends. That the demon spirits intend to execute that sentence. Well, I have some news for you, the priest, and all who entertain any designs of mischief toward me and my friends.

"As I told that spirit counselor last night, I have placed my friends and myself in the care of the Life-giver, the Christ of Calvary. And I'm prepared to walk under the shadow of death as long as Christ accompanies me through the presence of His Spirit."

Shocked into a state of terror, my friend could not speak for about a minute. His face turned white, his eyes became fixed, and I thought he would pass out.

"Are you OK?"

He did not answer.

"Roland, is anything wrong with you?" Still no answer.

Then silently I implored, "Dear Jesus, please help!"

Shaking his head, he said at last, "I don't know what happened, but it seems as though I lost consciousness for a moment. Morneau, I know that the Spirit accompanying you is great and powerful. Please don't mention the subject again. It terrifies me."

When he appeared normal once more, I requested that he carry my message to the high priest.

"I have not made myself completely clear regarding the ultimatum, Morneau. The threat on your life extends beyond what the spirits can do to you.

"The controlling committee has decided that your defection from our ranks could result in secret information, damaging to the cause of the master, leaking out. There was talk of having a contract put on you. One individual was willing to go as high as $10,000 to have someone do away with you. But we thought the suggestion unwise and turned it down.

"However, we did come to a decision. If a spirit informs us that you have spoken to anyone on the outside about the activity of our secret society, three individuals have volunteered to shoot you at a convenient time. The controlling committee felt that this would be a wiser move, seeing that it would be restricted within our society and we would thus avoid the possibility of becoming involved with the law.

"We brought the plan before a spirit counselor, and received full approval, along with the gift of clairvoyance for the volunteers so that they would know at all times where you are. I had hoped that I would not have to tell you this, but your refusal to comply with the high priest's wishes leaves me no choice. I'm sorry."

"Tell the priest that I'm daring, but not stupid," I replied. "I have nothing to gain by telling anyone about this secret society. Keeping my mouth shut—I can live with that. But for my survival to depend upon the word of a lying spirit—that I will not stand for.

"Tell the priest that I have a new Friend in the person of Jesus Christ. He is all powerful and commands respect. So much so that at the mention of His name demons tremble. And when commanded in that great name, even spirit counselors flee, as I witnessed last night."

I don't know whether what I felt could be called righteous indignation or not, but Roland's threat stirred up in me a determination to have him face the power and justice of God every remaining day of his life. "The priest seems to be knowledgeable about the Bible. Have him look up Colossians 2:9, 10. It spells out in black and white what I have been saying about the Lord of glory."

Quickly I jotted down the reference on a piece of paper so my friend would not forget. "And while he has the Bible in hand," I added, "I have something else for him to consider.

"Centuries back, a powerful king went about conquering and subduing great nations and people. But one day he insulted the wrong person. He attacked one who had made God a close friend. As a result he lost 185,000 soldiers. Only a few of Sennacherib's officers survived to witness the results of the king's boasting. And after he arrived home in Ninevah, two of his sons put a sword in his back. (See Isaiah 37.)

"Roland, inform the priest that he should give a great deal of thought before doing away with Roger Morneau, lest the intended destroyers become the destroyed.

"I will now lay down the rules of how the *game of extinction* will be played. And I am doing it with the full backing of my new Friend, who this morning revealed to me how He intends to solve my problem."

Roland's eyes widened, and I had his full attention. After I walked over to the table where my Bible lay open to the thirty-seventh chapter of Isaiah, I called him over to see something. I had underlined in red those verses I intended to memorize: 14-20 and 33-38. Showing him in written form the story I had just told him, I explained how the Holy Spirit had blessed my mind earlier that morning, causing me to open the Bible and become aware of how easily God could solve my difficulties. Then I read him a few verses.

"I can see where something like that could happen to us," Roland replied, obviously concerned.

"Yes, and the responsibility rests on the high priest. Tell him that the day he and his boys seriously entertain the idea of rubbing out Morneau, the Life-giver will pull the switch on all of his demon worshiping members, leaving only him alive to make the funeral arrangements. It could take place during one of their praise sessions to their false gods. Suddenly dead silence will fill the worship room."

By now Roland had sat down and lit himself a cigarette. Beginning to shake, he could not place his cigarette on the ashtray. I had to walk over and do it for him.

"Morneau, I have to go. I'm afraid that what you have just told me may take place if no one else but the priest knows about it. So I'm going to phone George as soon as I leave here and tell him about all of our lives' being in danger unless we stop those three self-appointed executioners. If the news gets to all the members before the priest has a chance to have me sworn to secrecy, there's a chance that the pressure exerted on him to call off the assassination attempt will be great enough to guarantee you a long life."

As I shook his hand for the last time, he stated that because he did not want to displease the spirits, we should avoid meeting again. If by chance we met anywhere we should ignore each other's presence. I told him to have it his way.

In that manner ended a tension-filled trip into the supernatural, and the loss of a close friend. But the benefits I gained by breaking away from it all have been many. The fact that I am still alive today testifies to the goodness, love, and power of the Lord Jesus to save.

I never met Roland again, but saw him from a short distance once when he came out of a store on Ste. Catherine Street West. Getting into his illegally parked Cadillac, he sported a white hat and what appeared to be a silk suit. He was impressive to look upon, but I did not envy him.

As I walked down the street that beautiful June day to catch a streetcar, my joy in the Lord was great. Raising my heart to the Holy of Holies of the heavenly sanctuary, I conversed with Him and truly considered the experience as being fullness of life.

Although I had turned my back on the spirits and all they had to offer, they kept trying to reestablish contact with me. Rappings took place almost every night and continued for months. One evening Cyril came to observe. After he heard their activity he exclaimed, "Let's get out of here. How can you stay in this place? Why don't you move out?"

Somehow I didn't want to give the spirits the satisfaction of thinking that I feared them. I figured that if I started to run from them I would have to flee them forever. Therefore I trusted in the Lord Jesus to provide me, wherever I happened to be, the help and protection I needed so greatly.

Chapter 14

Counting My Blessings

On that first Sabbath, when I was about to leave the Adventist church sanctuary, I asked the Lord to make it possible for me to find myself there again next week. And when I returned, I raised my heart to God in thanksgiving for His having worked in my behalf in the days just passed. In fact, the whole day was one of rejoicing in the Lord and of counting my blessings.

I then found by experience that great benefit to be realized by a person reviewing or counting his blessings. The commandment to remember the Sabbath to keep it holy I perceived to have been given in order to make it possible for man to escape the constant demands of the temporal affairs of life and thus have the time to count his blessings, and in that way be brought closer to the Creator and be refreshed both physically and spiritually.

After my confrontation with the spirits, and life for me had taken on a new normal pace, I immediately turned my attention to searching out in ecclesiastical and secular history how the Christian church had become involved in Sunday observance, had given the observance of the Biblical Sabbath, and had adopted such doctrines as the immortal soul and eternal torment. For a period of five months I spent almost all my leisure time at the municipal library of Montreal. With great interest I read the writings of the Roman Catholic Church in the light of Bible prophecy. I looked into the lives of certain saints considered pillars of the early Catholic Church and examined their influence on Christianity. The history of popes took on a new meaning, Origen of Alexandria, an early Greek church father living between the years of A.D. 185 and 254 who succeeded in uniting some of the philosophies of the eclectic schools of Neoplatonists with the doctrines of Christianity, especially fascinated me. That period of research and study served to solidify my belief in the Bible.

One beautiful Sabbath day in April of 1947 I had the blessed experience of being baptized by immersion into the membership of the Seventh-day Adventist Church. On that same day I met a young woman named Hilda Mousseau.

As some of us were leaving the church after the evening meeting, Pastor Taylor stated that anyone headed east could ride a couple of blocks with him to the place where he was going to park his car for the night. Four of us accepted his offer, and after reaching the pastor's destination, started for the nearest streetcar stop.

In that way Hilda and I became acquainted, and a number of times after that walked to the streetcar together. It wasn't long before we found that we had common interests, likes, and dislikes. After a while we found ourselves going steady.

One day I thought it would be a good idea to try to convince her that she should become my wife. In those days it was a major project for a fellow to ask a young woman to marry him. He had to consider what would be the right place and time. Reviewing my plan of action a number of times, I set my sights on a particular Sunday evening.

The important question would have to be brought up under relaxed conditions. An ideal time to ask would be while we waited for the night watchman to come and unlock the door for Hilda. It always took two or three rings for the man to arrive, amounting sometimes to 10 minutes, depending on how far away he was in the building.

Hilda was then working as a nurse at the Montreal Convalescent Hospital and resided in the nurses' quarters of the hospital. All resident nurses had to be in by 11:00 p.m. The closer one returned to that time, the shorter the wait. Therefore I figured 10:30 would be ideal.

It was a beautiful June day. As planned, we had an enjoyable Sunday afternoon and evening together, culminating in a tour of the city of Montreal in an open streetcar.

After each stop, as the tramway-car would pick up speed, Hilda's long blonde hair would raise from her shoulders and float in the breeze, and her blue eyes would sparkle as they reflected the light of the many neon signs along the street. The more I looked into her face, the more convinced I became that her name should be Hilda Geraldine Morneau.

About 10:30 that evening we approached the entrance of the nurses' residence, and like many times before, Hilda pressed the bell button and kind of leaned her shoulder against the door in expectation of the usual long wait. Immediately I asked her whether she would consider marrying me. No sooner had I spoken the words then the watchman appeared. Unlocking the door, he walked back about ten paces, folded his arms, and stared at me with an air that seemed to say, I dare you to give her a good-night kiss in my presence.

Both my question and the quick arrival of the usually slow moving watchman took Hilda by surprise. She stated that she had thought about the matter and had expected that it might take place in the distant future. Now I assured her that all I was looking for at the moment was a Yes answer and that we would discuss it later at a time more convenient for her.

No sooner had I said that than the watchman barked out, "Young lady, are you coming in, or do you want to stay out there? I got work to do, and if you don't come in I will lock the door with you out."

She gave me a quick Yes, a peck of a kiss, and rushed in almost in tears.

"I'm going to teach you girls that when I unlock the door it's for you to come in then," the man snapped.

"It's not every night," she replied, "that a girl is asked by a fellow to marry him."

The watchman looked startled. "I'm sorry," he said. "Why didn't you tell me it was that important. I would have given you more time."

Hilda determined then and there that she was moving out. Her mother had an apartment on Queen Mary Road, and Hilda decided to live with her regardless of how far she would have to travel to work.

At the same moment I headed home feeling foolish that my timing had been so way off.

As soon as Hilda could reach a phone, she called her mother to inform her of her plans. "Mother, I have something wonderful to tell you."

"You do—what is it about?"

"I am going to get married."

"Are you out of your mind? You're only 21. Besides, whom are you going to marry?"

"I'm getting married to Roger, that young man from church who I have been going out with. You know, the one you met a couple of times."

"Yes, but you have known each other only a short while. Aren't you rushing things a little?"

Then, according to Hilda, the fountain of tears let loose and she began to cry her heart out. The conversation closed by her mother's saying there was no need of crying—they would talk things over when they got together.

The next evening when I called Hilda, she informed me of her mother's viewpoint on the subject. I suggested that we both go and visit her mother on the coming Sunday, and I would ask her for Hilda's hand in marriage. We would discuss the important matter with her and work things out to a satisfactory conclusion.

It turned out that her mother was quite understanding concerning our intentions, and we chose the evening of September 20 for the wedding.

It wasn't long before summer gave way to autumn, and the latter sought to outdo its predecessor in warmth, beauty, and charm. I rose early, the Sabbath morning of our wedding day, to discover all of nature vibrant with life. By the time we came out of church after the morning services, the thermometer had reached 80 degrees. A few dry leaves floated in the gentle breeze.

Friends of ours by the name of Ruth and Arthur Cheeseman opened their home to us for the wedding ceremony. We planned it to be a quiet occasion with only a few close friends attending. Among the guests were two SDA clergymen and their wives: Andre Rochat, minister of the French church, and L. W. Taylor, minister of the English church, who officiated at the ceremony.

Mrs. Cheeseman, Mrs. Mousseau, and the other ladies had beautifully arranged the home for the occasion. As my bride and I repeated our marriage vows before the pastor, I stood tall and straight. Not to impress any of the friends present, but because of the many invisible beings looking on: angels who had come from the presence of the Almighty to rejoice with us, and demons—commanded, I believed, to attend by their heartless leader, who had seen their diligent efforts turn into failure when by the grace of the Lord Jesus I had walked out of their ranks.

Besides, I was wearing my best suit—that tailor-made one I had bought with the money I had acquired playing the horses with the aid of the demons.

Epilogue

Forty-seven years have passed since my involvement with the supernatural world of evil spirits. I am now advancing in age and on the threshold of the eighth decade of my life.

The fact that I am still alive, I believe, is because I have been under the care of the Life-giver, Christ the Lord of glory. To decide for Christ at the age of 21, when the spirits were offering me wealth, fame, and power, was the wisest choice I have ever made. And to have a solid relationship with Christ, and like the apostle Paul, to "be found in him, not having mine own righteousness . . . but that which is through the faith of Christ, the righteousness which is of God by faith: that I may know him, and the power of his resurrection"—all this has brought into my life a wealth of peace, contentment, and joy in the Lord that no amount of money could ever buy.

As I told in my recent book, *More Incredible Answers to Prayer*, were it not for His power of love, cancer would have sent me to the grave in 1989. In addition, God has been blessing in glorious ways the prayer ministry He has led me into. The Spirit of God has been transforming lives, remedying seemingly impossible situations, and providing solutions and victory for the hopeless. Let me give just one example.

A friend wrote to Hilda and me and asked us to pray for her husband, who was facing surgery for the removal of a kidney. Because of the man's age and the fact that he had suffered a stroke six months before, the doctors feared that he might not survive the operation. Yet they could not allow the cancerous kidney to remain in the body.

As so many times before, the Spirit of God sustained my faith in the power of Christ's resurrection, and I asked my Lord that if it would be to the glory of the Godhead, would He please cause the power of the "Spirit of life in [Him]" (Rom. 8:2) to permeate our friend's body and drive away the elements of death that were destroying his kidney.

When the man woke up the day before the operation, he felt so well that he wondered out loud if he really needed the surgery. After a series of tests, the physician found, to his great surprise, that the kidney showed no sign of disease, and the large tumor that had been attached to it was gone. The following day he was discharged from the hospital.

Having such prayers answered is worth far more than anything the spirits could have offered me. All I can still say is, *Glory to God in the highest!*